SIDELIGHTS
ON THE
CATHOLIC REVIVAL

SIDELIGHTS
ON THE
CATHOLIC REVIVAL

by

FRANCIS J. SHEED

Essay Index Reprint Series

ILLINOIS CENTRAL COLLEGE
LEARNING RESOURCES CENTER

BOOKS FOR LIBRARIES PRESS
FREEPORT, NEW YORK

INTERNATIONAL STANDARD BOOK NUMBER:
0-8369-2176-3

LIBRARY OF CONGRESS CATALOG CARD NUMBER:
74-99649

PRINTED IN THE UNITED STATES OF AMERICA

CONTENTS

FOREWORD

This book was nearly called "Our Own Trumpet."

It is a selection from the articles which have appeared in our house organ "This Publishing Business" during the last twelve years.

I wrote the articles in the first place to sell books. In republishing them, I do not overlook the possibility that they may still sell books. I mention this to save readers the trouble of discovering it for themselves.

Why, you ask, should you pay good money to buy a book whose purpose is thus openly mercenary?

Why do you buy any book? For information, edification, entertainment, or to prop a table-leg. But a book may very well inform, edify, entertain or prop a table-leg even if part of its purpose is to persuade you to buy other books.

In the last twelve or fifteen years there has been an unusual amount of good writing by Catholics, so that it has been no exaggeration to speak of a Catholic Literary Revival. The present moment, when war seems likely to diminish the flow, is a good moment to look back over it. These articles were written for the most part as the manuscripts came into our hands. They touch on almost every great name in the movement, and on the principal elements that gave the movement its special quality. Some of the essays treat of books no longer in print: they are included either because the book was of importance at its moment, or because the essay happens to treat of a notable man or an important principle.

F. J. SHEED

SIDELIGHTS
ON THE
CATHOLIC REVIVAL

KARL ADAM

The last decade of Pius IX's reign (1868-1878) was not a flowering time of the Catholic Intellect. Newman was in his prime, but as he looked about him he saw almost no one else. For the glory of that decade was in the cradle, and the cradle guards its secrets closely. (What secrets may our own cradles be guarding at this moment? None, probably: those of you who are alive in the seventies will know.) But considering what the adults of that day were, it is pleasant to think of little Paul Claudel born in 1868, little Hilaire Belloc (1870), little Gilbert Chesterton (for he could have given small hint of his present bulk in 1874), little Henri Ghéon (1875) and little Karl Adam (1876)— to say nothing of little Thérèse Martin (1873), who also in her convent at Lisieux was to write a best seller.

Of all these, the one upon whom Newman's own mantle has fallen is Karl Adam, who has achieved so notable a pre-eminence in the New Apologetic, that his name is taken as synonymous with it, and the word pre-Adamite applied, not more than half-jestingly, to what has gone before. So far as I know only one photograph of him has ever appeared in this country. Be on your guard against that photograph. It is doubly misleading: for the proportions of the head suggest a giant of a man, and he is short and thickset; and the collar suggests a layman, whereas he is, these last thirty years and more, a priest.

His life, apart from his having thrice been driven out of professorial chairs, has not been eventful. He was born at Pursruck in Bavaria, one of the ten children of a teacher in the national schools. He studied philosophy and theol-

ogy at the Theological College at Ratisbon. After his ordination in 1900 he did two years' work as curate in a parish,
work in which he revelled and for which, if we may judge
by certain glorious stories that are still told of him, he had
a special aptitude. But already as a student he had caught
the eye of his professors and he was sent off to the University at Munich to pursue his study of the history of
dogma. In 1917 he went to the University of Strasbourg as Professor of Moral Theology. When, in 1919, he
was driven out of Strasbourg by the incoming French, he
was given the Chair of Dogmatic Theology at Tübingen,
where there are two Theological Faculties, one Catholic,
one Protestant. He was deprived of his chair shortly after
Hitler's advent for a very outspoken speech on the Jewish
contribution to Christianity, was re-appointed almost immediately, and later deprived of it again.

Karl Adam has stated his purpose with great succinct-
ness—"to render the spirit of Catholicism intelligible to
the contemporary mind." Every word of this phrase is
worth weighing. It expresses all that has made him the
standard bearer of the New Apologetic. He does not seek
to prove other people wrong, nor even to prove Catholicism right, but simply to render it intelligible. The essence
of the formula is in Newman but it *could* not be applied
in all its purity in Newman's day: some alloy of controversy there had to be. But there is no controversy in Karl
Adam—save in his more technical works on the development of dogma: here he has had much learned controversy
with other Catholic scholars, particularly upon the Sacrament of Penance in the Early Church. But the books he
has addressed to the world at large are purely positive, all
illumination. On a later page his great Christ trilogy is

discussed in some detail: and no more need be said of it here. But two things are worthy of note: (a) he relies absolutely on the power of the truth itself to hold the reader; there is no epigram, no paradox, not the hint of a joke; but hold the reader he certainly does; (b) his work is for Catholics as much as for non-Catholics: it is to render the spirit of Catholicism intelligible to "the contemporary mind"; and if we Catholics think of the contemporary mind as a disease from which other people suffer, we are twice wrong, for it is *not* a disease (though it is in part diseased), and sound or unsound it is largely our own.

ON BEING ONESELF

Being oneself is a difficult feat. Everything is against it. There is the pressure from outside—the state deciding our education, advertisers deciding what we shall eat, drink, smoke, read and wear. If there is any part of us left un-standardized by those external agencies, it is attended to by the consuming flame of our desire to keep up with the Joneses.

> *Father's in the pig sty,*
> *You can tell him by his hat,*

says the old song. We're all of us in the antheap, and you can tell us by—well, what *can* you tell us by? Not by our hat: we should never dare to wear a hat that was not worn by millions of other ants. Not by anything that we can manage to mould into conformity. Free and independent? We exercise our freedom in a steady refusal to be inde-pendent—a refusal which becomes positively panic-stricken if independence is urged upon us too insistently. One's first reaction to the title of Daniel Sargent's new book, *Four Independents,* was surprise that there should be so many. And, in fact, three of them are dead.

They are a curious collection, these four. Orestes Brown-son—the only American in the party and the longest dead —was a Catholic philosopher who insisted on being him-self (to be anything else is death for a philosopher) at a time when philosophy among Catholics had reached its lowest ebb. He had a contemporary—Newman—with the same odd bee in his bonnet. Neither of them got much fun out of it. They would have been happier now.

4

The other three—Péguy, Hopkins and Claudel—are poets. At first glance Péguy is the most interesting. Hopkins was a revolutionary in metre and in diction, but we are used to revolutionaries in those fields (though not, be it noted, to revolutionaries who are satisfied to write and not concerned to be read; had it not been for Bridges, England's late poet laureate, we might never have heard that there had been a poet called Gerard Manley Hopkins). Claudel has his own views in a field of thought and a field of art in which most of us do not even have other people's views. But Péguy! Even if we do not read his poetry—even if, reading it, we do not know why to so many Frenchmen he is "notre Péguy"—the general detail of his life is an expression of the solitary self to the point, or past the point, of eccentricity.

Is it a coincidence that all four became Catholics? Daniel Sargent does not think so. The Church is the permanent home, and is fast becoming the only home, of personality. She even irks her own followers by her insistence that they be themselves: and when men leave her it is invariably because that demand of hers has become too great a strain. If you say that that is a paradox, we must argue the matter at some time more convenient.

These four men anyhow are very Catholic and *very* independent. So, indeed, is Daniel Sargent who draws their likenesses.

THE CITY OF GOD

The Communist who matters is a man who has seen a vision. If you want to know the essence of his vision, Our Lady said it two thousand years ago:

> *He hath put down the mighty from their seat,*
> *and hath exalted the humble.*
> *He hath filled the hungry with good things:*
> *And the rich he hath sent empty away.*

It will go ill with us if we fail to see its splendour. For we shall go on meeting the Communist with our solemn arguments, showing this fact by statistics and that fact by psychology, confronting this statement of Marx with that statement of Stalin and both with some rigmarole from the local Communist party platform, destroying all his foundations with the ruthlessness of our common sense— and leaving him as firmly grounded as before, but angry with us and more passionately in love with his vision than ever. You cannot destroy a vision by nibbling at it or laying violent hands on it or throwing stones at it. You cannot meet a vision with arguments at all. You can meet a vision only with a vision. And we have one—one that includes the Magnificat—a vision of which the Communist's vision is actually one ray. The unanswerable answer to the Moon is the Sun: for the sun does not contradict the moon but accounts for it and to show its superiority has but to show itself. So that it should be easy for us. They have a vision but we have the Vision! But it is our tragedy that we have got used to our Vision—centuries and centuries ago. We scarcely think in terms of vision at all: visions are visionary; and we are as sensible as any agnostic.

Use and custom have dulled the edge of the wonder of Catholicism. We even lay it as an accusation against the Communist that he is a visionary. For with all the Sun for our birthright we are cold, and they are aflame with their small ray.

This dimming of vision has not in us been complete. Some doctrines have held their radiance—as the Blessed Eucharist. Some have suffered more than others: but the greatest sufferer of all has been the Church. Read back and see how the Fathers apostrophised the Church, how the mere thought of the Church filled them with a joy bordering on ecstasy: then think of our own cooler gaze. They saw her as the bride of Christ adorned for her bridal, we see her dusty and a little soiled with earthly polity. We see her through a haze of Popes and Bishops—saintly Popes obscuring our vision almost as much as bad Popes. We scarcely see the Church for her members. We go to her to receive God's gifts of grace and truth: and we do not see that she herself is God's greatest gift of all. Just as Christ is God as well as man, and too many see only the man; so the Church is Christ as well as men, and too many see only the men.

That is the great importance of Gertrud von le Fort's *Hymns to the Church*. Here is the Mystical Body of Christ as no *poet* has seen it for centuries. Here is no routine respectful Catholicism. Here is a powerful Catholic mind prostrate in the dust:

I have fallen on the law of your faith as on a sharp sword
Its sharpness went through my understanding, straight
through the light of my reason
Never again shall I walk under the star of my eyes and on
the staff of my strength.

She sees the living splendour of the Church, for the Church is Christ living in His members:

But strength still goes out from your thorns, and from
your abysses the sound of music
Your shadows lie on my heart like roses and your
nights are like strong wine.
I will love you even when my love of you is ended.
I will desire you even when I desire you no more . . .
Where my feet refuse to take me, there will I kneel down.
And where my hands fail me, there I will fold them.

She sees the powers of this world pathetic in their littleness:

You throw nations down before you that you may save
them
You bid them rise up that they may work their salvation.
See, their boundaries are like a well of shadow in your
sight and the roar of their hate is like laughter,
The clash of their weapons is like tinkling glass and
their victories are as tapers in small chambers.

She sees the scattered truths of mankind, and the Church able to complete even those truths which know nothing of her:

All the wisdom of man has been learned from you.
You are the hidden writing under all their signs.
You are the hidden current in the depths of their waters
You are the secret power of their enduring.

Nor is her vision only of power and majesty: the Church speaks to her children on another note:

He has come over me as buds come on a spray, he has
sprung forth in me like roses on the hedgerows.
I bloom in the red-thorn of His love, I bloom in all my
branches in the purple of His gifts.
I bloom with fiery tongues, I bloom with flaming
fulfilment, I bloom out of the Holy Spirit of God.

We must meet the Communist vision with a vision: and men are so made that the most radiant other-worldly vision will not dim the radiance of a vision of this world: but with the Church seen as Gertrud von le Fort sees her, we have a Kingdom on earth to set against their kingdom on earth. Yet it is not only to counter Communism that we should see the Church as she is: but because she is what she is and we are what we are. And it may be, in God's providence, that the mission of the Communist with his flame is to remind us that our own fire is burning low.

A WORD ABOUT CLAUDEL

Catholic novels have got themselves a bad name, so that even Catholics avoid them. Why? Not, we think, for the reasons usually given. It is not simply that too many of them end with a flurry of wedding-bells and a shower of conversions. The reason is more fundamental. The Catholic as a Catholic has been taught that God is everywhere and that all things are overruled by Providence: he has been taught it and he believes it. But he sees the hand of Providence best when things fall out as he would have arranged them if he had been God! So that as a novelist the Catholic too often takes his little section of life, and instead of seeing Providence in it, he acts Providence to it. As you read you feel that the whole thing is being manoeuvred.

The supreme model for the Catholic artist is Claudel's immense and possibly un-presentable play *The Satin Slipper*. He has taken an enormous slab of life—Spain and its new world, lust and murder and worldly wisdom and sanctity, piracy and martyrdom—and he does not manoeuvre it one inch. He takes for his clue the Portuguese proverb "God writes straight with crooked lines": and he amplifies this to read: "*All* things minister to a divine purpose and so to one another. Even the falterings of circumstance and the patternings of personality, *sin and falsehood*, are made to serve truth and justice, and above all salvation, in the long run."

Claudel's huge success in so huge an enterprise makes *The Satin Slipper* the most influential Catholic work of art of this century and many before it. It is necessary to read the play at least twice, for one is a little dazed the first time: and as it takes quite a long time to read, you may feel that so many hours would be too much to devote to an experience so improbable as that of feeling the wind of the Spirit blowing in the unruliest actions of men.

CHRISTOPHER DAWSON

There was once a University graduate who thought that Socrates was a Roman. He not only thought it, but said it. And, on being corrected, explained that his subject was Sociology, not Classics. Thus it emerged that he did at any rate know that the Classics are concerned with Romans and Greeks. But apart from this chance gleam of general knowledge, this one flaw in the otherwise perfect integrity of his specialisation, he was an excellent symbol of that tendency to divide the kingdom of the mind into separate departments which began its work of ruining education four hundred years ago.

This departmentalising, of course, can never be complete. Let a man be never so much a specialist, some things outside his subject he cannot help knowing or half-knowing. And here comes in another fact—the human passion for synthesis. The mind will not see things as isolated units, but must have them in one picture, and so seeks one unifying principle which will make them cohere. If the mind is not wholly in touch with reality it will take a part for the whole, and this is the disease of the "Omniscientists" of to-day. Hence the violent crudity of the main syntheses attempted within the last life-time—the evolutionist synthesis, for instance, which was very rapidly absorbed into materialist atheism, and walked hand in hand with the economic interpretation of history and the communist theory of life. All these bear the unmistakable mark of a false synthesis—a total ignoring (or a rabid denial) of some field of human experience; and what these ignore is the most important field of all, the spiritual. The result is disaster. A defective synthesis arises from a narrowed vision, and narrows the vision still further. Materialist atheism, for instance, did really mean to elevate man by removing God: and in so far as it got rid of the conception of beings superior to man, it left man at the summit of the universe; but it was a shrunken universe, and the shrinkage bids fair to bring all man's powers of action to a standstill.

This necessity of a new synthesis, based on a view of the whole, is the truth Christopher Dawson maintains in everything he writes. What is particularly to be noted in him is the immense range of his knowledge. In *Enquiries into Religion and Culture,* a book of his collected essays, he writes with mastery on the most diverse things: Islamic Mysticism, Confucianism, the Donatist Schism, Bolshevism, Sex; he has written the best short book on the religion of primitive man,* and an even better book on the Dark Ages.† Set down like this, it is calculated to make our Sociologist-who-had-heard-of-Socrates shudder. But Dawson is not another H. G. Wells innocently breezing about in fields where better men walk with care. He writes in every field with assured knowledge, how acquired I cannot conceive, but unquestionably derived in some way from that clear view of the whole which once was, but has not been for centuries, the object of every educated man.

* *The Age of the Gods.* † *The Making of Europe.*

THE SIEGE IS OVER

Over the Bent World, the Modern Catholic Anthology
compiled by Sister Mary Louise, is a book of some 750
pages, containing 147 pieces of prose and verse written by
74 different authors—American, English and Continental
—all of whom were still living within the last ten years.
The selection is a good one and the Catholic Literary
Revival is thoroughly represented.

Naturally, given the great variety of Catholics, there is
a great variety of notes in the book from the gentlest half-
whisper to the roar of a Belloc. But the dominant note is
certainly wit, humor and high spirits. You get the impres-
sion that Catholic authors stride through the land gay and
confident. So might a victorious army march with all its
battles behind it. Yet Catholics are a minority, barely
emerged from persecution.

Note also that this is true only of those who write in
English. There is no such wit or gaiety among the French
or German Catholic writers. Voltaire has no successor as
a wit in French Catholicism, whereas there are three or
four writing in English who could match him jest for jest.
Continental Catholic writers are profound, moving, beautiful, but not notably gay. And they never play the fool.

My theory is that the special quality of English Catholic
writing traces back to Newman's great controversy with the
Protestant Kingsley. You remember it vaguely perhaps.
Kingsley had said that Catholic priests taught that truth
was not a virtue and instanced Father Newman as a priest
who had actually taught this. Newman replied. Kingsley

14

replied. After further interchange, here is Newman's summary of the controversy:

"Mr. Kingsley begins then by exclaiming: 'Oh, the chicanery, the wholesale fraud, the vile hypocrisy, the conscience-killing tyranny of Rome! We have not far to seek for an evidence of it! There's Father Newman to wit;—one living specimen is worth a hundred dead ones. He a priest, writing of priests, tells us that lying is never any harm.' I interpose: 'You are taking a most extraordinary liberty with my name. If I have said this, tell me when and where.' Mr. Kingsley replies: 'You said it, reverend Sir, in a sermon which you preached when a Protestant, as vicar of St. Mary's and published in 1844, and I could read you a very salutary lecture on the effects which that sermon had at the time on my own opinion of you.' I make answer: 'Oh . . . *not*, it seems, as a priest speaking to priests; but let us have the passage.' Mr. Kingsley relaxes: 'Do you know I like your *tone*. From your *tone* I rejoice,—greatly rejoice,—to be able to believe that you did not mean what you said.' I rejoin: 'Mean it! I maintain I never *said* it, whether as a Protestant or as a Catholic!' Mr. Kingsley replies: 'I waive that point.' I object: 'Is it possible? What? Waive the main question? I either said it or I didn't. You have made a monstrous charge against me—direct, distinct, public; you are bound to prove it as directly, as distinctly, as publicly, or to own you can't!' 'Well,' says Mr. Kingsley, 'if you are quite sure you did not say it, I'll take your word for it,—I really will.' 'My *word*!' I am dumb. Somehow I thought that it was my *word* that happened to be on trial. The *word* of a professor of lying that he does not lie! But Mr. Kingsley reassures me. 'We are both gentlemen,' he says, 'I have done as much as one English gentleman can expect from another.' I begin to see: he thought me a gentleman at the very time that he said I taught lying on system. After all it is not I, but it is Mr. Kingsley who did not mean what he said."

This was the first time that a Catholic had fought back. Catholics had, of course, replied to arguments before. But this time a Catholic seized his man and with the best humor in the world shook him till his teeth rattled. Kingsley was as shocked as a hound would be if the fox were to turn and rend him. This was not Catholic-baiting as the game had been played in England for centuries. It was a superb moment. And I think it accounts for the phenomenon I have noted, what can only be called the take-on-anybody, don't-care-a-straw note of English Catholic writing—men writing not arrogantly as if they own the earth but all care-free because they know who owns it.

ROSS HOFFMAN

Ross Hoffman's biography does not take long to outline, partly because he is still in his thirties, mainly because having chosen his furrow he has kept steadily to ploughing it. The serious student has no time to acquire a biography. Ross Hoffman was born in Harrisburg, Pennsylvania. He is now Professor in the Graduate School at Fordham. In between lie studies (at Lafayette, Columbia and Pennsylvania State), a couple of trips to Europe, marriage, a Professorship at New York University, conversion to Catholicism. There is not much external action, but plenty in the mind.

What is first to be noted of him is that he *is* a historian. His book *Great Britain and the German Trade Rivalry* won the prize of the American Historical Association for the best monograph of the year on European International Relations. His path to the Church was very much the path of history. History it was that forced him first to look at the Church, then gradually to see her; and for him conversion is simply a seeing process. "The faith," he writes in *Restoration*, "is a reality to be recognized, not a thesis to be established." But history is not an end in itself; it is an equipment. For what?

Notice the names of his godfathers in the Faith. He was most helped, he says, by Karl Adam, Belloc, Dawson, Maritain and Chesterton. These are the makers of the most modern Catholic mind. If those are your godfathers, you must belong to the thirties of the twentieth century. The generation they have done most to fashion has not yet produced many writers. Hoffman is one of the first. As such he would be significant anywhere. But his immense significance is that he is an American. Influences from abroad can only flow fruitfully into a country through a man of that country, and he must be of the requisite stature. If the best European Catholic thought is to make itself at home in America, it must take possession of one or more American writers. It would be difficult to be more American than Hoffman. His eighth grandfather back came from Germany in 1739 and the family has been in Pennsylvania ever since. He is of the necessary stature. European thought comes not to fill his mind like an empty box, but to colour and deepen his own original thought. Equally, if any American Catholic is to make a contribution to European thought, Hoffman seems likeliest. Europe has already begun to take note of him. That, then, is his significance. He is the American who stands on the frontier between America and Europe. If I am right!

What gives Ross Hoffman his special appeal as a writer is his eloquence. It is not rhetorical. But his writing has a lift and a drive in it, rare in the rather nerveless writing of the present day. And this is as it should be: for what he stands for precisely is a renewal of vitality. Things, he feels, have not so much gone bad as gone slack. The evils that lie in wait for Western Civilization are not dangerous in themselves: we shall fall into them not because they are overwhelmingly strong or overwhelmingly fascinating, but because they lie at the end of the line of least resistance. They are to be combated not by any direct attack upon them, but by a re-vitalising of ourselves. Even before he joined the Church, he was repelled by the flabbiness of alternative Causes. Pacifism for instance—"lacked the justification of any really worthy purpose *and made little call upon my will* to serve something better and worthier than my own selfish interests"; of his Socialistic days he writes— "It seemed to me that we did not care enough for victory. There were no timeless and priceless values that we were willing to defend against the price of a little more comfort"; the Liberals "like the Stoics mean well but have not heart enough for a real revolution. They recognize nothing actually worth dying for."

The restoration of vitality is then *the* task. How do you restore anything to vitality? By re-uniting it to its roots. There in one word is his mission. America is full of virtues, religious and civic, dying because they have broken away from their roots in history. These roots lie on the other side of the Reformation. It is not of course the Middle Ages that he would bring back, for they too were fruits and not roots. But "the spirit that animated them was immeasurably fertile and timeless, capable of penetrating the body of any civilization and restoring it to life and health."

KNOX'S BIBLE

If any word has a more truly Protestant ring to it than
the word Bible, it is the word Knox. The odd chance
which gave Father Ronald Knox the same surname as
Calvin's gloomiest child inspired Chesterton's quatrain:

> *Mary of Holyrood may smile indeed*
> *Knowing what grim historic shade it mocks*
> *To see wit, laughter and the Popish creed*
> *Cluster and sparkle in the name of Knox.*

Perhaps it may restore John Knox's equanimity (if he
is in a place where equanimity can flourish) to find his
namesake producing an edition of the Bible; but if he
is still a Presbyterian, his satisfaction will be ill-judged.
Whatever use he put the Bible to in his lifetime, its true
use is within the Church. The Biblical attack on Catholic
dogmas did not (after the first shock of the attack) destroy
Catholic attachment to the dogmas; but it sensibly weak-
ened Catholic attachment to the Bible. A man can never
feel quite the same about even the nicest book if he has
just been beaten round the head with it.

Naturally this feeling would not last in full force for
ever; there are still, of course, Catholics who look on
the Bible as dangerous to faith, but the majority got over
the feeling soon enough. Or rather, not soon enough. For
in between had come an immense change in men's reading habits. Printing, which was pretty well as new as Protestantism, had multiplied books; more books to read meant
less time for any one book; the large new literate but
uneducated public developed the grand game of reading
for pastime; and Catholics who had slackened off Bible-

reading out of an obscure fear that it might be dangerous to their faith, now failed to resume Bible-reading because it was too solid for their taste. This Scriptural insufficiency of Catholics is the last heritage of the Reformation still to be liquidated. Liquidated it must be. How necessary Scripture is to the life of Catholics, St. Jerome indicated long ago with his phrase "Ignorance of the Scriptures is ignorance of Christ": and if we might feel inclined to elbow him aside as a specialist naturally enthusiastic for his speciality, Pope Benedict XV has made the phrase his own. The question is not whether the restoration of Scripture is necessary, but how it can be done.

It is in an effort to answer this question that Father Ronald Knox has produced his abridgement and re-arrangement of the whole Bible. As it stands the Bible contains something like a million words; it is in seventy-three books, not arranged according to any apparent system. To the man approaching it, it looks rather too much like a jungle. Father Knox has reduced it to about a third—it is now about the length of a long novel, but nowhere near the length of *Gone With the Wind*. He has concentrated on the story of God's most fundamental dealing with the human race, omitting what has a less direct bearing on that, occasionally re-arranging the order. In the words of the Archbishop of Westminster's preface, he has produced a ground plan of the whole Bible. The jungle looks a little more like a garden.

THE RETURN OF THE GIANTS

Men who in music and poetry will have none but the masters are in their spiritual reading satisfied with writers of the standard of Ella Wheeler Wilcox—at this standard a great deal of spirituality is written: reading some of it is like chewing a mouthful of fur.

This double standard is not the incredible disharmony it might seem, for even the least excellent Catholic writing does contain the word of God, and two grains of the word of God, cluttered up with ever so many mediocre words and images provided by the human writer, can storm the mind more powerfully than "Hamlet" or the Fifth Symphony. All the same, there is a certain penuriousness in reading only the lesser moderns; and fortunately in our own days we are seeing the return of the Giants. St. Thomas was the herald of their return. Eyes clarified by him peered into the mist from which he had so lately been dragged, almost violently, by Leo XIII; behind him loomed vague and shadowy the figures of St. John of the Cross and St. Augustine, and over them the mightier figure of St. Paul, and over all, the Gospels. The mist still shrouds a hundred other figures, but these are the giants. These a Catholic owes it to his own maturity to know. The Bible, one fears, will return but slowly; and its full return will mark the true dawn for the Catholic Intellect: "When the incomparable music of the Bible has been an integral part of an education," says Fr. Martindale, "all other literatures for ever seem to lack an essential grace." Meanwhile the others make progress—or we make progress towards them. St. John of the Cross first: so much has Pius XI accomplished that few remember that it was he who declared St. John of the Cross a doctor of the Universal Church; yet it is doubtful if anything else he has done will equal this in long-reaching effect. There is an admirable translation of the great Carmelite's works by Allison Peers: for those who would approach him more gradually there is *The Mystical Doctrine of St. John of the Cross*, an arrangement of passages from his own writings to present the essence of his thought.

St. Augustine remains; and it is strange how timidly we approach the most human of the giants (he who, when young, prayed to be freed from his sins, "but not yet"). No one who has thought much upon the Thomistic revival can have failed to see that Augustine must return too if Catholicism is to save the world. Here even more than with St. John of the Cross, the gradual approach is necessary, for the bulk of his writings is enormous. Everyone *must* of course read the *Confessions*. But after that *The Augustine Synthesis* arranged by Fr. Przywara, S.J. will lead the reader into the very heart of the Master of all the Doctors. It would be endless to set down all that this man who saw the break-up of an age-old civilization has for our own generation. Here there is no space for more than a word on the elementary experience of merely reading him. It will take a while to become acclimatised to his way of writing, which is not so much difficult as unlike the prose we have grown used to, the prose which has given rise to the adjective prosaic, and even to the adjective prosy. This is what Fr. Martindale has to say of the writing and the writer: "To the end his body would remain wiry, short, vibrant. And to the end his mind leapt and pounced and ricocheted from notion to analogy, from phrase to assonant word, from tiniest grain of thought to remote association of idea. It must always have been his difficulty to *resist* the hurricane-swift alliance of ideas, and keep to what he was really talking of. For him an idea almost instantly suggests its opposite—he tosses it away only to recatch it before it has escaped him; he inverts it, he inserts it—who knows how: the result is not only true but limpid. Augustine could hold no mere frozen idea before his mind—the thing palpitated forthwith and came to life and he hated it or loved it. If there was intellect in his mysticism, there was passion in his philosophy. And with it all, was that strange, enduring tenderness of heart, such that unconsciously he swerved, lest he should weaken, towards taking the harder course, sometimes with others, always with himself."

HILAIRE BELLOC: A CHARACTER OF THE REFORMATION

Anyone who reads Belloc's *Characters of the Reformation* must feel that Belloc himself would have fitted into that gallery. The vitality that marked the men who made or fought against the Reformation is in Belloc himself. There is a quality in him which everyone feels, and feels to be inexpressible. Perhaps it is this: that one can imagine him as living in *any* period of history and affecting the issue of things. Try that test on almost any other living writer you can think of: a few can be imagined in this or that rather tired age—Bernard Shaw might have shone in the eighteenth century, but not in many others; some are so nondescript that any age would do as well as this, though in earlier ages they would probably not have been taught to read and write at all; the mass of them are plain twentieth-century provincials, born of this age, and unthinkable in any other. But Belloc—in what age would he have been at a loss? or different? or unregarded?

From the feeling that he would have fitted into that gallery of Characters of the Reformation, came the sudden realization that he belongs to it. When the whole history of the Reformation comes to be written, from its inception (whenever that was) to its final liquidation (whenever that may be), Belloc will be seen as a powerful factor in its unmaking.

His life-work has been the finding and telling of the truth about the Reformation. Other men have been busy in the same field; but who are they? Who knows more than their names? Belloc had the power. What Belloc writes, goes *home*: they could no more ignore him than they could ignore a tiger on the doorstep. He has dealt with one aspect or another of the Reformation in a score of books: in *Characters of the Reformation* he summarizes the whole. The Reformation from its beginning to the stabilization of Protestantism in its present boundaries was a matter of two hundred years. In an introductory essay which is a real *tour de force*, he surveys these two hundred years while the issue sways uncertainly and shows who were the men whose actions and counter-actions combined to produce the stalemate. In the remainder of the book he shows just what each of these men counted for: and how little any of them counted beside the two great considerations—the determination of the rich to hang on to the looted Church property, and the determined placing of national interest before religious.

This, in fine, is the accomplishment that will give Belloc a place in history. Let Protestantism be as noble a thing as a Wesley or a Hooker could make it; yet it remains true that no great religion ever had so shabby a beginning. No Protestant now glories in the Reformation. Yet within living memory they gloried in it. What has happened in between? Belloc: it is he who has made it impossible for any literate person not to know what sustained its beginnings. And the man who destroys a movement's pride of origin, has planted death in it.

PLASTER AND SANCTITY

A friend, glancing through one of our seasonal Lists, remarked that whereas we were apparently bringing out two saints' lives in one season, *he* did not read more than one in ten years.

Nor is there any doubt that in this he spoke the mind of the *ecclesia discens* as it has been for the past 1,900 years. We are oddly reluctant to read of people in whose company we wish to spend eternity. The reason, since it certainly does not lie in the saints' lives, must lie in the saints' Lives: in the steady growth of a special tradition as to how this particular sort of work should be done—a tradition grown so rigid that to the casual reader one saint looks exactly like another, and the subjects of the various biographies might as well have been called St. A. and St. B., for all the personality that at first sight emerges through the mass of flattened history, miracles without number and sheer bad writing.

The last is the most obvious: it was cliché, but cliché in superlatives, commonplace phrases on the very tips of their toes. The result was a style of writing strained, unnatural, overloaded, as though the writer, feeling the inadequacy of ordinary speech, had decided to talk falsetto.

And then the miracles. It is not that we do not believe them: we take it for granted that a saint worked miracles, as we take it for granted that he breathed. But miracles, while overwhelming to see, are not always very exciting to read about, and it is a pity to drown a saint in his own miracles.

The flattening, as we have called it, of history, is much

more serious. The biographer had his own notion of what
a saint should be; anything that did not fit that notion was
made to fit it. His object being to edify, he brought a very
vigorous hand to bear on what did not edify *him*, and attributed motives, and invented states of mind, and had a
very confident knowledge of much that could not well be
known.

The evil of all this can, of course, easily be exaggerated.
Occasionally the resultant picture is entirely false: to place
under a statue of the traditional St. Aloysius his own
phrase, "I am a piece of twisted iron; I entered religion to
get twisted straight," could provoke nothing but laughter,
and a feeling that he had got twisted very straight indeed.
But for the most part, with all their faults, saints' Lives
made great reading: the personality of the saint was so
strong that for whoever read closely it broke through all
the well-meant artifice, just as the personality of Ste.
Thérèse triumphs over the massed cheapnesses of the Car-
mel chapel at Lisieux.

Sentimental prosing about the saints is bad, but the reaction has its dangers. One reader urged us to produce a
series of "Lives of Saints by Profane Laymen," and France
more particularly has lately seen one or two specimens,
written apparently with the object of picking up anything
the Devil's Advocate overlooked. The authors are probably
seeking the truth, but with a gleeful hope that it may be
scandalous when found. This transplantation of the Lytton
Strachey method is great fun—a new game to play; but
there is something of the edged tool about saints, or it
may be the two-edged sword.

The truth is that if a man does not write a saint's life
on his knees, he will make nothing of it. He should not be

constantly pointing to his knees or drawing public attention to his clasped hands, but an immense reverence is
vital. Given that, two things seem to be required: first, that
the writer should be aiming at the truth, sparing no labour,
since it is only from the facts that the saint himself can be
known and not from a mixture of psychology and guess-
work, shirking nothing—since the most unpleasant truth
is more edifying than the most edifying falsehood; second,
that the writer should be able to write.

If anyone is still curious to know what all this means, let
him read, say, Henri Ghéon's *Curé d'Ars*, Alice Curtayne's
St. Catherine of Siena, and the symposium *The Irish Way*.
We believe most firmly that the best introduction to
Catholicism lies in the lives of saints, not only because in
them you have essential Catholicism, but because the
saints are of a sort to interest that huge outside public
which is quite certain that it has no interest in sanctity.

STERILISED THINKING

In Douglas Woodruff's *Plato's Britannia*, Socrates, visiting the England of our own day, makes first for the Athenæum, and there finds men engrossed with a crossword puzzle. So early in his journey he could not know that here was almost a perfect symbol of the disease that has come upon modern thought, particularly in religion and philosophy; yet so it is. *There is a furious activity of thinking, and in the same minds a distaste for truth definitely discovered* (whether called dogma or certitude or some other name) as for something likely to hamper thought. Yet truth is the object of thought, as colour is of sight, or sound of hearing. To glorify the activity and undervalue the object of the activity is folly; and that is precisely the folly of our generation.

It is clear enough how this is symbolised by the crossword puzzle—which means very considerable mental activity and no truth discovered, or even discoverable, as a result; for the end of such a puzzle is no new truth, but merely an arbitrary arrangement of what was already known—an arrangement in itself valueless, and, once achieved, not valued.

I do not want to seem to be attacking crossword puzzles: I have myself failed to solve several. I am not attacking the pastime; I am only wondering why a generation whose whole thinking is of the same sort should regard it as a recreation, when the essence of recreation is change.

For the moment, then, thinking is in the ascendant, and truth, or dogma, or certitude—which are only other names for *successful* thinking—are terms of contempt. It is a form of birth control in the sphere of the mind, activity divorced from its object, assured of sterility. As such, it is certain to be fatal, not only to truth, but ultimately to thinking itself. For men will pursue an activity while not desiring the object of that activity, only if the activity is pleasurable. But real thinking hurts; only certain colourable imitations of it are entirely pleasurable.

What is to save our generation from thus going out of its mind? A return to a philosophy in which all man's activities are co-ordinated—each subordinated to its own right end—all together subordinated to the right end of man. Scholasticism is such a philosophy, and Jacques Maritain has written an *Introduction* to it—not for professed philosophers only. For it is the great and unique glory of scholasticism to be a philosophy for all men. All men are *by nature* scholastics. Let them but learn it and crossword puzzles will once more be of their lives a thing apart and not their whole existence.

FRANÇOIS MAURIAC

François Mauriac deserves the most serious consideration of all students of the Catholic Novel. In his youth he was a devout Catholic, and wrote a book of poems which for all their quality (Mauriac never wrote rubbish) were yet related definitely if distantly to the *bondieuserie* school of religious art. Then came a curious phase, lasting twenty years or more. He had not ceased to be a Catholic. He tells us that he always knew he could never be anything else. But he was not practising his faith, nor giving any particuar thought to it. He was formed as a novelist by influences external and even hostile to Catholicism: in particular he was influenced by Anatole France. With *Le Baiser au Lépreux* he took first place among French novelists, but readers would scarcely have suspected his Catholicism. Then, towards 1930, he rediscovered the Faith—or rather discovered it. The story of his progress at this stage is of poignant interest. Two articles in the *Nouvelle Revue Française*—*Souffrances du chrétien* and *Bonheur du chrétien* (which came six months later)—and a little book of Meditations on *Maundy Thursday* outline the story on the specifically religious side.

But such a change in the man had to mean something revolutionary in the novelist. With *Ce qui était perdu* the new influence was obviously present but not assimilated, the old and the new were not yet one single stream. Then came *Vipers' Tangle*, which stormed a position: it was a Catholic novel which forced the critics to discuss it simply as a novel.

The whole question of the Catholic Novel is too immense to be discussed here, but observe Mauriac's contribution to the discussion. The particular temptation of the Catholic novelist he expressed in three words, "falsifier la vie." Given his history, the hint is worth following up.

Mauriac was elected a few years ago to the company of the Forty Immortals, the Académie Française. It is a pleasant parable that he should have been given the place rendered vacant by the death of Brieux, whose *Damaged Goods* was the sensation of twenty-five years ago. The *New Yorker's* Paris letter, describing the ceremony, describes him: "Mauriac is now forty-eight, thin as a fashion plate, sallow-skinned, and armed with an enormous, well-bred, hooked nose. In his flashy Academician's uniform, he looked like an intelligent, unheard-of Southern king."

MEDIAEVAL PHILOSOPHY

The man who said that Benedictines have not been great philosophers because their motto is Pax showed more knowledge of philosophy than of Benedictines. For philosophy thrives on dissension. The best evidence of the Scholastic Revival is the meeting of any two Scholastics; the distinguished courtesy with which Mr. This adorns but does not veil his contempt for Professor That is a happy proof that their common philosophy is awake and alive. It has returned to the lusty quarrelsomeness of its youth. At any time from the Reformation on, a Catholic philosopher might find himself rent in twain by his fellows, but usually for the theological bearings of his philosophy, not as now for its philosophical roots or implications. Odium theologicum flourished within the gates, but odium philosophicum was reserved for the outsider—Kant or Hegel as it might be—who did not need to be comprehended to be hated. But now all the excitement is within the fold. One remembers the famous Reunion meeting where

The United Presbyterian he ventured to suggest
That the doctrine of the Calvinists was better than the rest;
Which aroused the wrath and anger of the Plymouth
    Brother who
Said he thought a Presbyterian no better than a Jew.

Now Monsieur Chose of Paris (who adores St. Thomas) regards Monsieur Tel of Louvain (who also adores St. Thomas) as more dangerous than any Kantian. When this new phase began, it would be difficult to say. Perhaps the advent of Blondel had something to do with it.

The nature of modern scholastic activity is twofold:

there is the strictly philosophic activity of those who within the scholastic framework are making their own study of the universe of Being or one of its provinces (Edward Watkin's *Philosophy of Form* is an example); and there is the interpretative activity of those who re-examine the Middle Ages. This has three main branches: the re-examination of St. Thomas to find if the traditional Thomism truly represents him; the study of other great mediaeval philosophers; the combination of these two in a synthetic study of mediaeval scholasticism as a whole. Consider an example of each.

The Intellectualism of St. Thomas is the work of Pierre Rousselot, most brilliant of French Jesuits, who was killed in the war. Written twenty years ago, it has had an unparalleled effect on the development of modern Scholasticism. It takes St. Thomas's fundamental doctrine that life's supreme value, its radical and essential good, lies in an act of the *intellect*; tries to find what this meant in St. Thomas's own mind, in a manner as startling to the opponents of Thomism as to many Thomists; and shows how, for man, it leads not to a diminution of reality but to the richest hold upon it possible to him. It is not without significance that the translator is Father James O'Mahoney whose own book, *The Desire of God in St. Thomas,* made so considerable a stir.

Ernest Moody's *Logic of William of Ockham* is a work of disinterment. Ockham was buried in the dreadful oblivion of a name, a few perfunctory lines in histories of the period, and a label. Ernest Moody claims that he was buried alive, surprisingly alive; and that the label was also a libel. He *was* a nominalist—but a nominalist in logic only—and this precisely because in metaphysics he was a realist. He was not the cause of the degradation into which philosophy fell; he was the last upholder of the true Aristotelianism. Porphyry would have quarrelled with him. Aquinas would not. We have said that he is surprisingly alive. The physical problems he chose for analysis come closer than those of any other mediaeval thinker to the speculative interests of *contemporary* science; he is "modern," and his solutions are of a sort to appeal especially to modern philosophers of science.

These two books are fairly difficult. They are for the philosopher. The third book—the mediaeval synthesis book—can be read by the larger mass of the philosophically minded. It is Etienne Gilson's *Mediaeval Philosophy*— which contains the Gifford Lectures delivered by him at the University of Aberdeen. It is, but only incidentally, a history of the philosophy of the Middle Ages. What he is concerned to show is that there really was a mediaeval philosophy, and not only a number of mediaeval philosophers; further, that this was a Christian philosophy; and since this phrase appears to be a contradiction in terms— for philosophy must proceed by way of reason, not by way of revelation—there is an analysis of the relations between the two terms establishing the possibility of metaphysic affected by revelation yet maintaining its own integrity, as well as an examination of the various philosophers of those centuries establishing the fact—"that the Middle Ages produced, beside a Christian literature and a Christian art, this very Christian philosophy which is a matter of dispute."

ON TRANSLATION

If the fact of the moment is that thought is beginning to flow freely from end to end of the Catholic world, then the man of the moment is the translator. But consider how difficult an art he practises. If thought is to flow through him, it must first flow into him and then flow out of him again. And this involves difficulties on two levels.

First, there is the purely linguistic difficulty: few men are masters of two languages. They are either insufficiently skilled in the language *from* which—and this is a deficiency more widespread than its victims realise—or they are insufficiently at home with the language *into* which; a dictionary can tell them what the words *mean*, but only living familiarity can teach the train of associations that every word carries with it.

The difficulty on the second level is harder to overcome. The commonest of all faults is slavish adherence to the phrasing of the original, so that one feels the cadences of the first language jostling the cadences of the second. This means that the man is translating the words, simply substituting one language for another. The first of the two things necessary has not happened—the thought has not flowed into him, but the words only. It is for the translator to study the words till the words drop away and only the thought that formed them is left. Then the thought proceeds to embody itself anew in *his* words. By this time, if he have any gift for the job, he has forgotten what the original words were, being wholly possessed with the thought. The lady who asked for St. Francis de Sales' *Design for Living,* when she wanted an English translation of his

37

Introduction à la Vie Dévote, would make an excellent translator,* for she had embodied the original idea in admirable English and had not kept the faintest trace of the original words. To say of a translation that it reads like an original work is not the highest praise. It is the bare minimum.

On what has been said so far, every educated man should be a competent translator. But competence is not enough. Competent writing will not get *any* book read. There must be style—that is, such ordering of the words that the thought comes through with the dew on it. Thought is translatable, but not style. Thought is polygamous—it can wed a hundred languages. Or, to abandon a metaphor that too rapidly becomes unmanageable, thought is pentecostal, in itself transcending the difference of tongues; the curse of Babel affects it, but only incidentally.

But style is inseparable from the words. It is born with them and dies with them. The translator can borrow his original's thought, but he must distil his own dew. And it is at least an arguable proposition that the one man in the world who cannot do that is the man who is equally at home in two languages. The bigamist does not get the most out of marriage, nor the bilinguist out of language.

---

* Though *Introduction à la Vie Dévote* would *not* be a good title for a French version of Noel Coward's highly immoral comedy.

THE VISION OF PIERS PLOWMAN

Curious that Catholics of the English tongue should have let so rich a piece of their heritage as *The Vision of Piers Plowman* pass from them. It is incomparably the greatest Catholic poem in the language—perhaps the only one, reckoning by the standards of world poetry; and no other standards are of application to William Langland. But he wrote in an English and in a metre that were to be submerged by the great flood of Chaucer, and within a century or two of his own time his fellow-countrymen could not read him. In modernising his poem, Professor Wells of Columbia has done something in one way comparable to the translation by Fitzgerald of *Omar Khayyam*. Probably *Piers Plowman* will not sweep the world like Omar; for it is not wrought in rose petals. But the anger of Langland is worth letting loose again upon a world still full of those evils which first provoked it.

For Langland is a man in a rage and his rage has the one thing that makes rage fruitful—its first object is himself and his sins:

So I live without love, like a low mongrel
And all my body bursts from the bitterness of my anger.

But his own self and his own sins do not exhaust the rich store of his anger, and we have as a consequence such a picture of a world out of harmony with the will of God as it would be hard to parallel. On one side is the Trinity, and the virtue of Charity, which should bind men to the Trinity and to one another. On these two themes he writes superbly, coming back to them again and again. On the supremacy of charity he writes one of the greatest lines in any poetry:

Therefore Chastity without Charity shall be chained in hell.

On the other side is the world of men—churchmen and laymen, rich and poor—all classes corrupt and corrupting—charity unhonoured. What is to be noted throughout is the unflagging vigour of his writing. From end to end of the poem (two hundred and eighty pages of it) a storm is blowing. There is wit in plenty, but wit without mirth. Where, he asks, is charity?

> *In a friar's frock he was found once*
> *But that was afar back in Saint Francis' lifetime.*

When the great preacher comes from his most moving sermon on mortification and gorges at the dinner table:

I wished heartily, angrily and eagerly
That this same Doctor would devour dishes and platters
And they be molten in his mouth, and Mohammed in his belly!
I'll ask this bottle-bellied bulging jordan
To tell me what penance is, of which he preached so finely.

The rich man who lets the poor suffer unaided rouses him to outburst after outburst:

When his corpse comes in his coffin to burial
I believe it will scent the soil with so pernicious an odour
That all others where he is lying will be envenomed with his poison.

Of the small shopkeepers with their petty cheating, he rages:

They are retail robbers and rent wrackers;
They eat what poor people should put in their bellies.

For realistic word painting—of Chaucer's quality and greater than Chaucer's—consider his picture of Avarice.

He was beetle browed; his lips bulged also;
He had two bleared eyes, like a blind hag,
His cheeks lolled like a leathern wallet;
The skin sunk below the chin, shivering and agued;
His beard was beslobbered with bacon like a bondman's
He wore an hood on his head, a lousy hat above it,
And a tawny tabard of twelve years' service,
Tattered and dirty and full of lice creeping
Unless a louse were a good leaper
He could never have crawled on a cloth so threadbare.

The poem contains a score of such passages.

It is absurd to write thus in not very coherent gasps about a work of such magnitude. But a coherent treatise on *The Vision of Piers Plowman* cannot be got into a couple of pages.

FROM PODSNAP TO PINSK

"And the other nations," said the foreign gentleman.
"How do they do?"
"They do," said Mr. Podsnap, "I regret to say, as they
do."

If you deplore Mr. Podsnap, you do well. But in noting
the beam in his eye we must not overlook the mote in our
own. For no one is entirely free of kinship with Mr. Podsnap; not even Dickens, who created him. Be as international as you please, yet there will remain one little instinct at the bottom of your soul which says that, at the end
of all things, foreigners are foreign. It is the heaviest handicap that faces the Church in her effort to teach the whole
world. Nationality is a splendid thing and enriches the
Church's life with the immense variety of its streams as
they converge in her; but Nationalism—which is a name
masking with its dignity the identical thing which is so
shiningly absurd in Mr. Podsnap—troubles and muddies
both tributary and main stream.

How is the Catholic to face the problem? He can scarcely
root all the race-consciousness out of himself. Only the
very unsophisticated will feel his blood throb at the word
Aryan: and the revivalist I once heard asserting that English was the language spoken in Heaven was not a profound
thinker. But love of country is a virtue, and national differences are a fact. An Englishman is not a Frenchman; he
is not even a German (the view that he is an Anglo-Saxon
is rabid nonsense and need not detain us). It is the most
delicate of problems, and no one is more likely to appreciate its delicacy than a Catholic writer living in Hitler's

Germany. Johannes Pinsk's *Christianity and Race* penetrates to the very heart of it.

Each race of mankind has its own psychological formation, its own way of getting at reality. This he establishes as a primary fact. He then considers two questions: How far have various race outlooks—Greek, Roman, Celtic, Slavonic, German—already influenced the form of the Church's life? How far can these outlooks legitimately receive concessions?

The answers to these two questions enable him to proceed to his main point: the fullest realisation of the racial urge towards self-expression can be made inside the universal Church and cannot be made outside it. The Catholic German will be more German than the Pagan German. The saint will be the most German of all. There is obviously no space here to trace out the proof Pinsk gives; but, as a plain fact, the saints have tended to be quite extraordinarily of their nation. There never was a more typical Englishman than St. Thomas More, a more typical Frenchman than St. Louis, a more typical Italian than St. John Bosco. W. S. Gilbert's hero who *"Might have been a Rooshan, or French or Turk or Prooshan"* was obviously not a Catholic. And when an American is canonised, the Ku Klux Klan may sing its *Nunc Dimittis*; for the hundred-per-cent American will have been found.

CHRIST AND SCHOLARSHIP

For the best part of two centuries the Gospel story has been under fire. Every line of it, down to the very *existence* of Christ Our Lord, has been—at some time or other, by someone or other, on some ground or other—denied. And some of those who were by way of accepting it have by their interpretations been more destructive than the hottest deniers. The whole thing had become, for the Christian of average literacy, utter chaos. Such bits of the jargon as reached his mind—logia, interpolation, Paulinismus, Q, Fourth Gospel, creative community—were something less than shafts of light. For most men there were only the two alternatives: to ignore criticism and cling tenaciously to the Four Gospels (which is what most Catholics and all Fundamentalists did); or to waive the question of the veracity of the Gospels altogether and treat them simply as useful tributaries to the individual's own rich stream of spiritual consciousness (the Modernist must pardon me if this is a misstatement of his view).

Obviously if these are the only two possibilities, the first is immeasurably superior: it relates the individual to a real Christ independent of him. But such a mass of intellectual activity as has gone to the critical study of Christian origins cannot be ignored, since serious minds will enquire how much of the traditional teaching on Christ is left standing. And it ought not to be ignored: what is constructive in it must be assimilated; what is destructive must be met and analysed, what is false in it countered, what is true assimilated as before. Even if it is chaos, chaos must be surveyed. For our generation the surveyor-in-chief is Léonce de

Grandmaison, who died while his magisterial work, *Jesus Christ*, was in the press.

It is, of course, not a book about criticism, but a book about Christ. In the author's own words, "The aim of this book has been to throw a clearer light on the person of Jesus." Of the three volumes, Volume II is the core of the work, being concerned specifically with Christ in Himself —His Person and His Mission. By way of preparation Volume I treats of the sources of our knowledge, and of the state—political, social, intellectual, religious—of the world into which He came. Volume III treats of His works —prophecy, miracles and the Church He founded. The treatment, therefore, is positive. But in the course of it, every theory of every considerable scholar—from the soberest to the most fantastic—is stated and analysed. Thus treated, criticism ceases to be quite the chaos it has seemed. There are, of course, wild men with wild ideas: learned men can all too easily be fools: specialists may lack horizon: but all that vast labour has not gone without profit. And ironically—or naturally, according to the point of view—the Catholic is the one person who can draw all the profit from it. He can make more of each new discovery than even its discoverer. For with the light that he already has, he can see it in its true bearings and relations.

G. K. CHESTERTON

The greatest of all Chesterton's gifts was his charity, and he carried it to a very high point; for he suffered fools gladly. Not just patiently, or politely, or as one kissing the rod; but gladly. This may not be the highest peak of charity, but it is the most inaccessible and least often scaled— very few even make the attempt; and in him it was the more remarkable because fools did not always suffer him gladly, and he suffered much from fools—to the point, indeed, of being taken for a fool. And this, I think, he enjoyed too.

From the beginning, the obtuse depreciated him: and they had three excuses. First, what he was saying was of extraordinary profundity, and not all literary critics are built to breathe at a great depth. Second, he certainly used paradoxes (though not as often as the critics thought; for a paradox is a statement which appears to contradict itself, whereas what were styled paradoxes were often enough statements which merely contradicted the accepted view). Third, he did quite often play the fool; he was a man of extraordinarily high spirits, and many of his flourishes were simply a flourish of heels; a more comprehending critic wrote of him that if he were teaching geometry, he would draw all his triangles with noses—and this would be a very admirable thing to do since the triangles would be none the less triangular and yet would certainly be gayer; he played the fool because he had some high spirits to work off; but pity the critics, for one of the marks of a fool is that he does not know when another man is fooling; and how can a man of no vitality understand a man with an excess of it.

This was the point made about Chesterton in one of the first articles to take him seriously—Wilfrid Ward's "Mr. Chesterton Among the Prophets." What he expresses there, Chesterton's admirers have felt ever since: when people disparage his writing, we know exactly what they mean, but we cannot explain to them why we exalt him. We can see their point *and* ours, they can only see their own: which Wilfrid Ward sums up as an application of the old saying that Truth understands error, but error cannot understand Truth. And that is a reminder of another old saying about Truth—"It will prevail." As the years have gone by, the cry of "paradox" has sounded less frequently: and by the time he wrote his "Apology for Buffoons," (in *The Well and the Shallows*), only the irreclaimable thought him one.

For what had emerged was the evident fact that he cared for truth profoundly: cared for it so profoundly that his huge hospitality knew this one exception: that nothing presented to him as true could have the hospitality of his mind till he had examined its credentials. Let a phrase he never so consecrated by custom or fashion, he took it to pieces; and when he had put it together again it looked so little like its old self that they called it a paradox. My own schoolboy admiration of the phrase "Plain living and high thinking" received a jolt from his plea for "High living and plain thinking," and from this jolt it has never recovered; and the time-honoured criticism of Dickens that he could not describe a gentleman is improved by Chesterton's addition "as a gentleman likes to be described." Similarly his key-ideas—that orthodoxy is more adventurous than heresy, that marriage is more romantic than promiscuity ("Marriage is a duel to the death which no man of honour can decline"), that virtue is colourful and vice pallid—

have come to seem as obvious now as they were startling when he said them.

I have not tried here to make any proper estimation of the greatness of one who must be ranked not lower than Newman. Such a judgment is for a writer to make, and not a publisher. This article must stand solely as an inadequate tribute from one of those whom he always appeared to suffer gladly.

WAUGH ON CAMPION

When we announced that Evelyn Waugh was to write a
life of the Jesuit martyr Edmund Campion, there was
something like consternation. Those who had read his
novel, *Vile Bodies,* could make no sense of the announcement; and *Black Mischief,* published after his conversion,
did not make it any more credible. One critic begged him,
almost with tears in his eyes, not to let himself in for
something that would be just about as cheerful as a wet
Sunday afternoon in Manchester (England). But the book
was written. Anyone who has spent a wet Sunday afternoon
in Manchester (England) or even in Manchester (New
Hampshire) can read the book and compare the sensations.

It would not be wild to call Edmund Campion the first
modern man in English history. I know that this is a
conventional term of praise applied pretty indiscrim-
inately. But I think it true of Campion (he was far more
modern than Sir Walter Raleigh, the likeliest of the rival
claimants) and anyhow I do not use it as a term of praise
but purely for description. He was of a twentieth century
cast; and as this is the kind of thing that appears more evidently in little things than in big (since big things tend
towards timelessness), consider the moment when Campion,
passing with his young Jesuit companion through Calvinist
Geneva, challenged Calvin's successor Beza to a debate on
religion—the loser to be burnt at the stake! This early
effort to give reality to debate is a joke in the modern taste.
Any of us might have done the same, with one minor exception: he did it in Calvin's Geneva while Calvin's stake was
still smouldering.

His courage indeed is the most astonishing thing about him; more astonishing even than his brilliance; and that was no small matter. As a student at Oxford he had won the close attention of Elizabeth; he had a standing among the undergraduates not unlike that which Newman was to have; he had the gift of words, in English and in Latin; when he became a Jesuit, Elizabeth offered him the Archbishopric of Canterbury if he would forswear the Pope. But his courage is *the* thing about him. They racked him three separate times. His finger-nails burst from his fingers. And when they asked him how he felt he replied: "Not ill, because not at all." In its perfect precision of phrasing, it recalls St. Francis's address to the red-hot iron that was to cauterise his eye. His was not simply a courage that held on tenaciously; it was a courage that seemed to inhabit a different department of his being. His mind worked on efficiently and cheerfully no matter what was happening to his body. When, still in agony from the triple racking, he was about to be condemned to death, his speech was the speech not only of an unconquered but of an untouched spirit, a speech calm and co-ordinated and unanswerable. "In condemning us you condemn all your ancestors." At a moment when we are calling most of the virtues of our ancestors into question, there is one of their virtues men still worship. It is courage. Campion had it.

HENRI GHÉON

There was once a big business man who said, "The Pope has a nice job, of course: *but what does it lead to?*" Henri Ghéon would scandalise that business man horribly. No self-made merchant would ever propose him as a model to his son. For Ghéon is quite unconcerned about *getting* anywhere, totally concentrated upon doing something. And even if the phrase "doing something" made our business man prick up his ears, they would fall limp again when he heard what the something was—"rétablir le va-et-vient entre le ciel et la terre"—to bring the citizens of earth into closer touch with the citizens of heaven (a poor translation, but there's the French: make your own).

To understand his childhood is to understand his life work. Born in 1875, brought up by a devout mother, Henri Vangeon lost the faith in his early teens: he was still at the Lycée at Sens, little more than a child, but an honest child. He would not pretend even to his mother that he believed when he no longer believed. Many things contributed to bring about the catastrophe—one stands out definitely in his own mind: religion was taught without life or understanding, not organic in itself, not in any possible relationship to the art and beauty which had begun to fill his mind.

His was a happy atheism. What the world had to give him he took. He meant to be an artist, but as art is not a living, not a certain living anyway, he decided to become a doctor. He studied medicine in Paris, and from 1901 to 1909 lived the life of a country doctor in his birthplace, Bray-sur-Seine. He wrote much verse and a play or so both during and after his medical career: painted, studied music, was in at the foundation of the *Nouvelle Revue Française,* travelled widely.

His mother's death was an agony to him, but it did not re-convert him: at her Requiem Mass he could still look on the Host at the Elevation, with the certitude that Christ was not there. The story of his conversion cannot be summarised. It occurred during the war (where he served four years). Intimately bound up with it was Pierre Dominique Dupouey, Lieutenant-Commander of a battalion of Marines. They met three times only, in the space of a few months. On Easter Saturday, 1915, Dupouey was killed on the Yser: by Christmas, if we may adopt Ghéon's own figure of speech, Henri Vangeon, the atheist, had given place to Henri Ghéon, the Catholic—l'homme né de la guerre, the man born of the war.

Already in the trenches he began to write. By the end of the war he knew what he was to do. He had lost the faith as a boy because he had not been taught it as a living thing. One prime way to teach it as a living thing was to show the saints—the people who had lived it most fully. And the art form which was most obviously close to life was the stage. He proceeded, therefore, to write plays about the saints. Since 1920 he has written over forty. In 1925 he founded the Compagnons de Notre Dame to act them. And he acts in them himself.

Do not for a moment think of him as a writer of nice little plays for Sunday performance. The man is a genius. Of the three of his plays published by us in English, *The Marvellous History of St. Bernard* and *The Comedian* captured thoroughly sophisticated London audiences, while *The Marriage of St. Francis* is in the class of the Giotto frescoes which suggested the English title. As it happens he is best known in the English-speaking world by his *Secret of the Curé d'Ars,* which is plain hagiography in form (though plain magic in fact), his *Secret of the Little Flower* and the lives of St. John Bosco, St. Margaret Mary and St. Vincent Ferrer. But he regards drama as his field and biography as an extra—sometimes a mortification, sometimes a luxury. He wrote the life of the Curé d'Ars under pressure from a publisher—and only agreed because he had already collected the materials while working on the curious three-volume novel he built round the Saint— *Les Jeux de l'Enfer et du Ciel.*

What is the secret of Henri Ghéon? It lies in the "va-et-vient entre le ciel et la terre" which is so much his concern. The supernatural is to him the normal. Original sin, diabolic temptation, the friendship of the saints— these for Ghéon are not simply doctrines to be believed, but plain ever-present facts. He does not *wonder* at the saints. He wonders at himself and at us, his fellow sinners. They are the norm. We are the odd and almost incredible variants.

CONVERSATIONS OF A SAGE

There are three stages in the mastery of a philosophical truth. The first is when one hears it explained by a teacher, and can see it; the second is when one can call it up in one's own mind, and see it; the third is when it has become absorbed into the very stuff of one's mind and one can see *by* it.

A tremendous amount of philosophy is written from the second stage. The writer knows his philosophy and is capable of applying it to particular problems as they arise. I say he *is capable* of doing so: and when called upon—for example by the necessity of answering a question, or preparing a lecture, or writing a book—he does so. But short of thus being reminded to be a philosopher, he just thinks like anyone else. He can take up his philosophy when he wants it, and lay it down when the occasion of its use is over. Such a man knows philosophy. He is not a philosopher. That name is reserved for the man who has reached stage three. There is for him no question of taking up his philosophy for some special purpose. It is so much part of his mind that it is automatically and without more ado included in *every* act of thinking.

It is the excellence of Jacques Maritain that he is in this sense a philosopher. This may be seen particularly well in *Philosophy and Progress* (a translation of his *Théonas*). For here he is not settling down to the development of one theme—which one can hardly do without having at least some of the external trappings of stage two—but rather roaming over the whole field of modern life, allowing an opponent to raise such difficulties as occur to him.

Throughout one feels how automatic and instantaneous is the philosopher's reaction. He has seen the answer long before he can say it. And as the opponent is a fully-furnished modern mind of the widest-ranging curiosity, the Thomist philosophy is given a superb opportunity to show its actuality.

That very actuality is one of the questions discussed, as indeed it must be. The critic objects that the Scholastic mind gave up thinking in the thirteenth century and took to repetition, and that the very notion of a closed philosophical system is repellent. The reply is in two statements: (1) "It would be a mortal sin to isolate truth in a lazar house of sloth. And I grant you that scholastic philosophers have often committed this sin—a sin to which the professor and the pedagogue are peculiarly liable." (2) "The thing that came to a stop in Aristotle was not the development of philosophy, but the genesis of the embryo, the *formation* of philosophy: so that after Aristotle, philosophy, being formed, could henceforth develop without end."

THE MYSTICAL BODY

The Reformation did more harm to the Church than any other of the great movements out of her; and only gradually is the damage being estimated. The obvious damage of lost provinces filled the whole horizon; yet the Church had lost larger provinces before. But with every great early heresy, if there was loss of provinces there was gain of truth. In combating the heresy, new depths of truth were exposed to light. With the Reformation it was different. Where earlier heresies had concerned the content of the faith (Trinity, Incarnation, Grace) this one concerned the rule of faith: not what is true doctrine but only how is true doctrine to be known. Therefore the whole point of the Church's reaction was an immense concentration on the rule of faith, since none of the individual doctrinal errors of the Reformers was as practically important.

Now a concentration on the rule of faith is in itself a good thing: but in a life-and-death fight, it is difficult to concentrate on the vital matter without some lessening of attention to other matters. In the defence of the *rule* of faith, the *content* of faith could not receive all the attention due to it. And one doctrine that was almost completely in eclipse was the doctrine of the Church as the Mystical Body of Christ. But the Rule of Faith struggle ended (though this was not seen at the time) with the Definition of Papal Infallibility in 1870. The Reformation had produced its dogmatic fruit within the Church. With this highly practical matter thus rounded off, the Church could turn her full attention to those more important dogmas which are the end to which Papal Infallibility is a means.

The return of the Mystical Body is a tremendous thing for the individual Catholic. Without it he cannot know a fraction of his true dignity as a Christian. Catholic Action is being based more and more upon it; so is the Liturgical Revival; so is Catholic Sociology. But what exactly is it? Mgr. Fulton Sheen answers the question in his book *The Mystical Body of Christ*. The first four chapters deal with the main elements of the Mystery itself, the indwelling of the Holy Ghost, the organic relation between Christ and the Christian. (We have already spoken of this word "organic." It has a technical ring about it; but Catholicism will not be understood till it comes completely into currency. It is the word of words in the true doctrine of the Church.) The fifth chapter is a kind of pendant to the first group, showing how this doctrine is reconcilable with the sinful lives of so many Catholics in high and low places. In the remaining eleven chapters, the central doctrine is shown in its relation to the structure of the Church, its members living and dead; the Mass and the Blessed Eucharist, and finally to the social crisis. For anyone who would know clearly and unconfusedly what is his right relation to this world and the next, Mgr. Sheen's is a book to read.

ART AND THE CATHOLIC

The Catholic Revival, still happily with us, has not gone forward all along the line. We have ·seen an immense new life in philosophy and in theology, matters directly of the intellect; but of the arts only in that one which is closest to the word-using intellect, namely poetry. Paul Claudel is a very great poet, and he is not a solitary peak but the highest of a chain. But in painting, sculpture, music we can show nothing comparable. It is not ridiculous to mention Claudel's *Satin Slipper* in the same breath as Dante's *Divine Comedy*; it would be impossible similarly to compare any modern Catholic with far lesser masters than Dante in the other fields. Even in architecture, though there is a stirring, we have not produced or looked like producing a Chartres, San Marco or Parthenon.

Related to this absence of creation by Catholic masters is the absence of a Catholic public skilled in appreciation of these things. We have an educated taste in the written word but not at all in the arts that dispense with words. It is possible for a Catholic to have a developed taste in poetry and talk like a Yahoo about painting or sculpture— not even knowing what the painter is trying to do, accusing him of lacking some quality which the painter would rather cut his throat than have. Most of us, it is true, do *not* talk like Yahoos about these things but only because we do not talk about them at all. Among educated Catholics there is almost no discussion of painting or sculpture or music, save in small specialist groups: the point is that interest and appreciation are not diffused over the whole Catholic body.

That is why special attention should be paid to Jean Charlot's book *Art From the Mayans to Disney*. Charlot has an all-round-developed Catholic mind. In the last war he fought in the French Army with the Foreign Legion. From that he went to the Education Department in Mexico. For years he did archaeological work among the buried Maya cities of Yucatan, and last year he was lecturing to the staff artists at the Walt Disney Studios in Hollywood. He is a notable poet and a very notable artist. Yet—to illustrate the point I labored at the beginning of this note—the one work from his hands that is known to most Catholics is the picture of Father Damien he made for John Farrow's book. One way and another he is admirably equipped to introduce Catholics to a field in which they ought to be, absolutely must be, but for the moment are not, at home.

Jean Charlot is aware that any artist who writes a book on art is poaching on the preserves of the professional critics—"whose oratory on behalf of their dumb friend the artist more than often irritates the latter." This irritation indeed stars the book from end to end. There is the conventional critic of the older school who "divides Raphael's work and studies it successively for its unbroken line, its subdued use of space, its geometrically oriented volumes, its insistent local color. Those aspects may be bared under the scalpel of the critics, like the liver and lungs of a beautiful woman under the scalpel of the surgeon. Yet the good public are within their own right to enjoy their women undissected and state truly that Raphael is the painter of virginal beauty." There is also the conventional critic of the newer sort for whom "The great eternal themes —life, death and love—are new 'complexes' with Greek aliases full of Germanic implications."

Charlot admits—unnecessarily, as we think—that the critics are his superiors in the handling of words but he claims one superiority for the artist-turned-critic—"the same advantage that the bug has over the entomologist— he knows his subject from the inside." And this is the book's greatest richness, his judgments go so deep because he has done the job himself.

The book is in a way a Cavalcade of Artists from the Cave Men up to our own moment. There is special emphasis on two matters—Mexican Art (Mayan, Indian and Contemporary) and Modern Art movements (Impressionism, Cubism, Surrealism and the rest). Thus it combines a sense of the general movement of art with special study of two sections, one very remote from us, one very close: and all the time it is getting at the principles—and even the techniques—which underlie all art. The reader may begin the book with no notion of what art is about. He will not finish it so naked.

LEON BLOY

In the ordinary novel we read about people as mediocre and anaemic as ourselves: in fact any given character might be oneself crawling across the page. After such reading, Léon Bloy's novel *The Woman Who Was Poor* crashes in our ears like an explosion: we seem to be watching not men but monsters. But the ghastly thing is that here too the people are ourselves—as Bloy sees us.

The truth is that Bloy sees life life-size. We habitually do not. As we look at the surface of human action, or an inch or two below, our vices and other people's look commonplace enough, merely a ruffling of the surface. Lust, for instance, has a pretty wide range: superficially it means no more than a nice little man getting nice little thrills or a nasty little man getting nasty little thrills. But there's nothing "little" about what is really happening in the bottom of the soul—the continuing strife between nothingness and Omnipotence. So Bloy sees it. His people are like planets and comets and dead suns and this is no exaggeration since an immortal soul dowered with knowledge and will is immeasurably more magnificent in itself and more catastrophic in its ruin than any planet. We are prepared to concede this as a fact but think no more about it. Bloy could never stop seeing it, or see it tranquilly.

Therefore his villains particularly seem monstrous. He makes us see the very maggots writhing in them—Poulot and his mistress, Isidore Chapuis and his—she looked like "a mop for cleaning mortuary slabs in a leper hospital." But what he calls "respectable people" are even more horrifying—perhaps because their resemblance to ourselves

61

is more easily seen. Gacougnol's heir, and the agent who passed Leopold and Clotilde's premises as sanitary, and the daily-Mass-going landlady grinding her tenants—all these would probably have looked normal enough to us if we had met them in the flesh. But here we meet them in the spirit and for the moment we understand the "delicious sensation" Bloy felt that day in 1897 when so many rich Catholics were burnt to death in the fire that broke out at a charity bazaar.

But with that we touch our finger on his one great weakness. He did not quite see that even mediocre people, even utterly depraved people—even Isidore Chapuis—are loved by God. Chapuis and Ballot and the rest do not repent: one almost feels that Bloy would have been disappointed if they had. "I should be ashamed to treat a mangy dog as God treats me," Bloy once cried. And that is exactly how he treats Chapuis. Yet if the one sorrow is not to be a saint (as Clotilde says at the end), then Chapuis is the most sorrowful thing in the book—far more so than Clotilde herself.

But this is a reflection that comes afterwards. While we are reading the most moving story of Clotilde Maréchal, we live in Bloy's world and judge with his judgments. To have read the book is "a revelation, like coming out of the void." For good or ill, Bloy had to write *The Woman Who Was Poor*. A critic has said that Bloy's words were like lava, and nobody blames a volcano for hurling its lava off its own racked chest. So Bloy wrote his novel: and it is a marvel to us that he ever slept quietly with all that monstrous life inside him; and indeed there is no reason to think that he ever did sleep very quietly either before or after writing it.

In Europe *The Woman Who Was Poor* has had a most profound influence on all writing throughout this century. In England and the United States the book started more quietly—after all it was different, and that is an awful handicap: if novels aren't all exactly alike, where are we? But if it started quietly it will not die quickly. I think religious novels in the English language will begin to show some effect of Bloy.

THE WILFRID WARDS

No man is a hero to his valet, because the valet is a valet. A great man is not less great in his shirt-sleeves. But to a small man he looks so. Biographers should not be small. Boswell wasn't. Lytton Strachey was. The test is absolute. Read any realistic biography you please. If the people in it come out smaller for being seen *en déshabillé* then your biographer is only a valet after all.

In Maisie Ward's book on her parents,* we find many people in their natural state. We see the poet Tennyson with his "Block up your ears, Josephine Ward, I am about to tell your husband an improper story"; Newman out driving with Hope-Scott, his face growing longer and longer at the endless stream of puns that poured from his companion's lips; Newman again, called upon to speak impromptu and breaking down, unable to finish so much as one sentence; Ruskin drivelling forth a lecture he had not bothered to prepare, and Cardinal Manning giving forth a lecture he had stolen bodily from the speaker he was introducing; old Ideal Ward roaring with laughter at Manning's invitation that he should come and spend an evening with him whenever he felt depressed; Baron von Hügel thumping the table and addressing Bishops and cabinet ministers as "you fellows"; Gladstone roaring with laughter at a vocal imitation of Manning, then recollecting himself and becoming doubly statesmanlike; Balfour embarrassed because a relation had indiscreetly told the truth about him; Leo XIII searching for his snuff box and

* *The Wilfrid Wards & the Transition,* Vol. I, "The Nineteenth Century," Vol. II, "Insurrection versus Resurrection."

pretending not to hear something he preferred not to hear. And we feel, at the end, as though we had been in the company of giants.

But it is not only individuals who are shown with their private faces. The Church herself is similarly shown. The Wards have for the best part of a century been in the unusual position of devoting themselves as laymen exclusively to the service of the Church. They began it with the terrible old man, William George Ward, who had "the mind of an archangel in the body of a rhinoceros"—the first of the Oxford Movement converts, with his thirty years of unrelenting, maddening, half-wasplike, half-lionlike warfare against the Newman he adored. His son, Wilfrid Ward, biographer in chief of the Catholic Revival in England, had thirty years of liaison work between Catholicism and the English mind. And Wilfrid Ward's wife, Josephine, one of the creators of the Catholic novel, began life under the shadow of Newman and the austere old Duchess of Norfolk, and lived to speak on the street-corner platforms of the Catholic Evidence Guild.

Such a family grows to a special kind of intimacy with the Church as a living organism going about its daily work—the Church, to return to a previous metaphor, in its shirt-sleeves.

This intimacy makes the atmosphere of Maisie Ward's book. Such a family likewise develops a special sensitiveness to the Church's changes of mood and method—a matter very relevant to the generations here covered; for, in a world where old stabilities were everywhere in dissolution, the Church was (half-unconsciously, it would seem) making readjustments on a grand scale. And the Wilfrid Wards were among the first to grasp what was happening.

MILK FOR BABES

Ignorance of St. Thomas Aquinas varies from that of the Belfast judge who admired his *Imitation of Christ* to that of the educated Catholic who does not read him because he does not care how many angels can dance on the point of a pin. Why should anybody be ignorant of him? It is not that he is obscure. St. Thomas himself perhaps exaggerated when he called the *Summa Theologica* "milk for babes"; it is not as easy as all that; but it is not so appallingly difficult either.

The trouble I think is twofold. First, the mere arrangement—objections stated, then answered, then a general statement of the truth; this repeated hundreds of times makes an uneasy kind of progress for the modern reader: his feet stumble in this strange rhythm. Second, the atmosphere: illustrations from a different age, arguments from a different mentality; breathing another atmosphere is an effort. Most of us buy a volume of the *Summa* and mean to read it; but the trouble of feet and lungs wears us down pretty quickly.

Father Farrell's ingenious notion* removes both difficulties. His plan is to write out each volume of the *Summa*, following the same order of thought but forging straight ahead in unbroken chapters and drawing all his illustrations from the life we know. He has begun with the second of St. Thomas's four volumes—of which the master-theme is the Ethical Law, but that Law seen for what it is, the necessary condition of happiness.

Happiness like freedom comes from doing what we

---

* *A Companion to the Summa*, Volumes II and III.

ought, not from doing what we like—save, exceptionally, when we like what we ought. Eating what we like, for instance, produces that negation of happiness which we call indigestion: and the rule is universal. *The Pursuit of Happiness,* then (that is the subtitle of this volume), is the search for the laws that should govern our conduct. St. Thomas does it magisterially in his own way; and because St. Thomas does it magisterially, Father Farrell does it so too.

It is surprising how vividly St. Thomas's principles come to life with the aid of illustrations that belong to our own day. "The very red face and thoroughly embarrassed manner of a young nun going into the family entrance of a saloon to cast her vote" is an admirable example of "erubescentia at the thought of turpitude," but it would have surprised St. Thomas. Conversely it is surprising how modern theories of behavior lose lustre when stated alongside St. Thomas's principles. Thus the various modern ways of interpreting the passions in terms of the purely physiological (Freud's simplification which traces all emotion to the master instinct of sex is one example) are seen in all their incompleteness beside the great scholastic insistence that passion is a phenomenon of the whole animal unit.

These two examples represent the whole book: every principle of St. Thomas is shown both in its modern operation and in contrast with modern theories.

The second volume treats of the individual virtues and the vices that go with them, so to speak. And Father Farrell (or is it St. Thomas?) has the rare felicity that he can make the virtues sound not only more virtuous than the vices (which no one can deny that they are) but more vital than the vices (since it requires greater vitality to go up a hill than down it), and even more attractive and happifying than the vices.

It is a common belief—which even Catholics do not wholly escape, since it is in the atmosphere and it takes very exceptional nostrils to breathe part only of an atmosphere and repel the rest—it is a common belief that the road to heaven is paved with lost opportunities of enjoyment. When Catholics are tainted with this view, they console themselves with the reminder that the enjoyments of heaven will doubtless make up for it. But virtue is not of that sort: the relation between happiness and doing what one ought is absolute, so that there is no way of having the one without the other. This is the teaching of theology: and certainly all past experience seems to confirm it, however much we may hope that future experience will belie it! But we have never seen a book which hammers in the truth as this one does.

VITALITY AND SANCTITY

Henri Ghéon, as we have seen, is the society portrait-painter *par excellence*. He paints only the Best People. He paints Saints. Why does he thus restrict himself? First, to avoid monotony: men are in their essential personality irreducibly diverse: but sin blots out the distinctions and reduces the diversity: sin drains out the color of the man (which is his own and inimitable) and replaces it with the color of sin which is common property: all sinners look less like themselves and more like one another.

Second, to secure vitality: his kind of painting demands unlessened vitality in the sitter: sin, being a following of the line of least resistance, inevitably lessens vitality. Virtue of course does not mean the absence of sin: it means the right direction of energy. To quote Chesterton:

> *If you think virtue has languor*
> *Just try it and see.*

The sort of "virtuousness" which avoids the wrong direction of energy because there is no energy; there is a mere nullity.

All this is obvious: the Saints are vital, colorful persons. But not all of them look it. Even some of Ghéon's sitters only look it because he is a great artist. But one of his recent sitters, St. John Bosco, could not look anything else, no matter who the artist. He is a blaze of life and color. At the age of five he began to teach the other boys their catechism: every lesson ended in a free fight: "He had come to bring peace, and lo, there was war. In the name of holy truth he tore into battle." At ten he still taught catechism but held his audience by a display of juggling, conjuring, and general acrobatics which would have been notable in a man and in a self-taught boy was sheer magic. Twenty years later he persuaded the governor to let him take all the convicts in the city prison out into the country for a day's picnicking—without guards of any sort: they all returned unconstrained to their prison at the end of the day; he no longer needed even conjuring tricks to hold men, for in between he had conquered himself, had subdued the blaze of his temper, and could hold men by his own strength.

He began with the overmastering resolve to work for the souls of boys; and began with a handful of them in a tumbledown shed. In 1854 he founded the Salesian Order for this work primarily. A few years later he founded an order of nuns to work similarly among girls. He worked nineteen hours a day, talked much with Our Lady, was persecuted by atheists, government officials, even ecclesiastical authorities, above all and mercilessly by the Devil. He revolutionized pedagogical method. "What the memory of Don Bosco really clamours for is not a book, but a film —an immense popular film, packed with adventures, games, dreams, miracles, with fields and vineyards, sordid slums, shameful hovels and all the misery of soul of children abandoned to their own perversity; and over all the great pure breath of joy that came from the lungs of the little farm boy and scattered the mists."

The work spread through Europe, to South America, to Asia. Last year—eighty years after the foundation of the Salesian Order and forty-six years after his own death— there were seven hundred houses of Salesians with some ten thousand priests, and seven hundred houses of Mary,

Help of Christians, with eight thousand nuns. Since the early Franciscan days there has been nothing to rival so rapid a growth.

"His age," says Ghéon, and it is true of our age too, "choking with the pride of its inventions, refusing to accept God on faith, clamoured for results." John Bosco gave them results with a vengeance.

COMPARATIVE RELIGION

The man of two hundred years hence who has to write a thesis on twentieth-century religion will have much fun (if in that happy future fun is allowed to creep into theses) about the devastation wrought by Comparative Religion in the simple faith of college students. The young Christian comes to college, believing, shall we say, in baptismal regeneration. He learns from his Professor that ritual cleansing is mentioned in the Upanishads, the Rig-Veda, the Zend-Avesta, the Code of Hammurabi and Aesop's Fables; and that water figured in the religious exercises of the ancient Egyptians, the Druids, the Zulus, the Iroquois, and the Dog-Men of Darfur. These instances are chosen a little wildly, but the Professor would almost certainly not know a Upanishad if he saw one and hasn't a notion where Darfur is. Anyhow, the student speedily drops his belief in baptism and goes in for Companionate Marriage.

Comparative Religion is wrecker-in-chief for the faith of our own generation as Darwinism for the two generations before ours. Nor can it be said that Catholic writers have met the situation with any dazzling success. With one or two exceptions, they have concentrated on showing the uniqueness of Christianity by watering-down the resemblances of other religions; and this is a weary, endless task: because, with three or four thousand years and three or four hundred races to play about with, research is always bringing new resemblances to light: and each new resemblance has to be watered down afresh, to the discouragement of the Catholic teacher and the derision of the pupil.

In *The Religions of Mankind* Otto Karrer, a German priest living in Switzerland, lifts the whole question on to a different plane. He teaches quite simply that because man is everywhere man, and God is always God: and because man's striving towards God is something God will never leave unassisted: there will and must be, in all religions whatsoever, true values—that is to say, resemblances to Christianity. What would really be shocking would be the picture of man reaching out to God in all his thousands of religions, and God ignoring him.

The uniqueness of Christianity does not depend on God's having ignored the countless millions who have lived and died before it or outside it: it does not depend at all on what Christianity teaches or practises: it depends on the uniqueness of the Incarnation, on the Godhead of Our Lord and the organic relation of the Church to Him. Obviously, what is absent or incomplete elsewhere will find its completeness here: but the one thing by which Christianity is incomparable is its organic relation to God-made-Man. Thus we have the two related facts: the One True Religion founded by God: and the myriad religions made by men and, because they represented a striving for God, aided by Him, and therefore in various measures showing forth both true beliefs about God and religious practices in harmony with the deepest nature of man.

Once the religions of mankind are seen like this the difficulties vanish. Since the uniqueness of Christianity no longer depends upon the deficiencies of other religions, the discovery of new resemblances outside cannot affect our belief in the Church: and does deepen our sense of God's love for man and His providence working in all mankind. Dr. Karrer's book thus truly marks an epoch. It came to us with the recommendation of Karl Adam: and it does for the relation of the other religions to Christianity what *The Spirit of Catholicism* did for the relation of the other Christian bodies to the Catholic Church.

RETURN TO THE TRINITY

Nice in minutiae, careless of immensity;
connoisseur in instants and stranger to eternity;
accurate in hair's-breadths, incurious of infinity;
deep-read in Wells and witless of the Trinity.

That is a poem, the whole of a poem, from Robert Farren's book, *Thronging Feet*. He calls it "The Fool," and we Christians at large may feel happily that the last phrase lets us out. But if we are not "witless of the Trinity," we often *sound* witless when we talk about the Trinity.

There was once a Catholic business man who set out to expound the doctrine of the Trinity to a friend. The exposition was incoherent and earnest and ended with the phrase "Thus, you see, three is one and one is three." The friend being on the Stock Exchange yet knew enough of the elements of mathematics to recognize that neither statement was true: three is not one, nor is one three. To which the Catholic replied, "Ah, but that is the mystery." In which, of course, he was wrong. What he had stated was not a mystery but only a muddle. He knew as little about the Trinity as the Oxford Theologian who said "I am not interested in the arithmetical aspect of the Deity."

The distinction between a mystery and a muddle is worth noting. What God has revealed is mystery; as God's revelation lies in the average lay mind it is muddle. God Himself never asked us to believe the nonsense that many of us do believe. That we accept it is a proof of heroic faith: or perhaps of intellectual unconcern.

In either event it is unfortunate. Mysteries are meant

for the enrichment and illumination of the mind, the doctrine of the Trinity more than any other. But a travesty of the Trinity is at best idle in the mind, doing no good and only harmless because not too closely regarded; while to those who cannot attain to intellectual unconcern it can be sheer torture (which is one reason, perhaps, why so many artists and such like lose the faith, feeling the travesties sheerly intolerable and not knowing that the mysteries are far other). Neither for the revitalizing of the minds that remain Catholic nor for the restoration of those unhappy souls who have thrown up the struggle is there any substitute for the dogma of the Trinity. Much is said of a Catholic Intellectual Revival. Its true name is the Return of the Trinity.

That is why we attach so much importance to Dr. Arendzen's book, *The Holy Trinity*. Catholic publishers are not "publishing blind": each one knows what he is at; though no two are *at* precisely the same thing. In the first ten years of our existence we were constructing the framework of our own publishing edifice: with *The Holy Trinity*, the framework was complete.

That, of course, is our own affair. But the Trinity is every man's affair. The highest truth about the Highest is the proper food for the mind; beyond it, the mind cannot go; without it, the mind cannot reach its own maturity. Dr. Arendzen does two things principally: as against the "three is one", "arithmetical aspect" nonsense, he shows precisely where lies the mystery; and on the hitherward side of the mystery, he shows how much there is that the mind can make truly (and exultantly) its own.

One final word. People tend to think many books are over their heads which in fact are only incompatible with their reading habits. This book is not as easy reading as Bernard Shaw, Walter Lippman, or P. G. Wodehouse. That is to say, it cannot be read at a hand-gallop. But read at half-speed it will yield all its fruit to anyone who can read at all.

EDWARD LEEN

It is a curious thought that as late as four years ago Dr. Leen was unknown to Catholic readers, or nearly. Ten years earlier he had written an article—in the *Irish Ecclesiastical Record*, I think—on the Priesthood of the Laity, which anticipated the whole flow of Catholic teaching on the subject. But ten years is a long time. And in between he had done nothing to draw the attention of the reading public. He was young—he is only in his forties now—he was a member of a religious congregation, the Holy Ghost Fathers, who are a name to conjure with in the missionary field but not widely known in England or America. When I first met him, he was Headmaster of Blackrock College in Dublin: and before I met him I had been told of him as a man who could write all the fundamentals of Scholasticism on the back of a postal card—or it may have been a postage stamp—I did not notice which, for I did not believe it anyhow. I do now.

When he ceased to be Headmaster, his principal work was the giving of retreats: and now we began to hear more of him. He preached retreats in convents; and the convents took notes and sent mimeographed copies to other houses of the same order throughout the world; and from all over the world nuns were writing to us to ask *when* would we publish a book by him. It was a new experience for us. No one has thus written about other retreat-givers. So it was that we published *Progress Through Mental Prayer,* followed by *In the Likeness of Christ,* crowned by *The Holy Ghost.* England was quickest to discover that a new spiritual master had arisen. America had taken him more quietly, but when the flood broke, it broke.

What constitutes his special appeal? Upon this all reviewers are unanimous. He is the most doctrinal of all modern devotional writers. He has fed his intellect on the church's dogmas and the joy of them has spread from the intellect to the whole of his soul. He has re-discovered the thrill of the two great sources—Scripture and Dogma, and his spiritual method is not to tell us about his own thrills but to show us what has thrilled him and leave it to do for us what it has done for him.

The question is too huge to be examined here. But this much may be said: as against all the battering that the Catholic mind has to stand from the world in which it is, nothing is so powerful as the nourishment of that mind by the revealed truth. Moral exhortation is not enough, nor a reliance upon the beauty or the tradition of the Church. The only true nourishment for the intellect is the truth. But this nourishing cannot be done by any mere outline of Catholic doctrine such as the Catechism gives. The Catechism is a splendid skeleton of truth: but it needs flesh and blood. By itself it is no more nourishing to the mind than the skeleton of a sheep would be to the stomach; and no more stimulating to the imagination and emotions than the skeleton of a film star. The flesh and blood comes from bending the whole mind to the discovery of what the doctrines mean and what life means and how life and doctrines are related. Some mighty instinct is driving the laity to the study of dogma. And no man now writing satisfies their instinct more than Edward Leen.

CHESTERTON AND ST. THOMAS

Nothing could better convey the purpose and method of Chesterton's *St. Thomas Aquinas* than the fact that throughout the book the comparison is between Aquinas and St. Francis—not Scotus, not Bonaventure. In other words, since this philosopher is compared not with other philosophers but with the least philosophic of men, it is clear that the author is concerned not with St. Thomas's importance to philosophy but with the importance of St. Thomas's philosophy to the world at large. In the light of that purpose, the book is a triumphant success. If you want to know precisely wherein St. Thomas differed from St. Bonaventure, you will not find it here. But if you want to know how St. Thomas's philosophy has affected every Brown, Jones and Robinson of us, then you will find it here as nowhere else. And many a philosopher will rub his eyes at this book to discover that philosophy matters.

St. Francis and St. Thomas, says Chesterton, must be seen together. His mind lingers on this unlikely pair—the large deliberate man and the small darting man: "While the romantic glory of St. Francis has lost nothing of its glamour for me, I have in late years grown to feel almost as much affection, or in some aspects even more, for St. Thomas." Affection for St. Thomas has been all too rare in the bleak deserts of admiration which spread around him to the horizon's edge.

"They were really doing the same thing. One of them was doing it in the world of the mind, the other in the world of the worldly. St. Francis used Nature much as St. Thomas used Aristotle. . . . *They both reaffirmed the Incarnation by bringing God back to earth.*"

With this last sentence as key, St. Thomas is shown in the middle of the stream of history, turning the stream. He fought for common-sense and sanity and the right to think. "He said what all common-sense would say if no intelligent heretics had ever disturbed it." He fought for the rights of the body against the Manichee. And Chesterton shows, as few men have ever shown, how all the apparently academic discussions about the One and the Multiple, about Act and Potency, about Mutability and Diversity, were in fact packed with dynamite, fraught with ruin to the mind if St. Thomas had not won. Of Being and Becoming, for instance, Chesterton writes "This distinction in philosophy is tremendous as a turning point in history." That, you think, is easy to say. One talks like that. But Chesterton sees it and makes us see it. Our own age has let go many of the fruits of St. Thomas's victory: and thought is damaged as he knew it would be. It is a great thing that the human mind should be turning again to the greatest champion it has ever known.

ISABELLA OF CASTILE

When Byron wrote —

There is a tide in the affairs of women
Which taken at the flood leads Lord knows where

he probably had not in mind either Isabella of Spain or Elizabeth of England. Yet both illustrate the phrase. There was a chanciness about the first beginnings of each of them, a long uncertainty followed by an immense success—and the same dubiousness about the ultimate issue. Isabella founded the Spanish Inquisition which kept millions in the Church—but which, by the very horror that has grown round its name, may well have kept more millions out of it.

It is one of the curiosities of our educational system that, as a rule, one is brought up with a fairly detailed if erroneous knowledge of Elizabeth, but without even a suspicion that the two greatest monarchs the world knew in Tudor times were Solyman the Magnificent, towards the end of the period, and Isabella of Spain at the beginning. Of Solyman just so much is known as can be gleaned from a footnote to the *Merchant of Venice*. Isabella is thought of as a mere flourish after Ferdinand, on the William and Mary model, while of Ferdinand (and Isabella) nothing is taught save that Torquemada and Columbus both worked for them.

It is probably the greatness of Isabella's own personality that makes the first fascination of William Thomas Walsh's book *Isabella the Crusader*. With such a woman, a book could not well fail. She took over the kingdom of Castile from the pitiful Enrique (by comparison with whose court Charles II's looks pious, and even Henry VIII's has a puritanical tinge) in as evil a condition as any State has ever been in: bankrupt, torn by the quarrels of nobles too powerful, everything in Church and State ruled by convert Jews of every degree of good and ill faith, the Moorish kingdom of Granada a heavy cloud to the south. She prayed and bore children and rode into battle: conquered Granada; brought back the rule of law; broke the great nobles; and firmly seized and solved, God knows whether rightly or wrongly, the Jewish problem.

But if it is her personality that dominates the book, it is by its own might, not through any feebleness in the issues involved. For two of the greatest of all problems of statecraft were in play—the question of absolute monarchy (with the sub-question that arises when the absolute monarch is a woman) and the question of religious toleration— of what to do with a large and unassimilable minority. She used the first to solve the second: she expelled the Jews; Spain must be one thing, and any foreign body that could not be genuinely and organically part of the unity had to go out altogether. Isabella did not mean to be unjust to the Jews, yet we can understand the Jews resenting her action. But whatever her actions may have been objectively, it may be doubted if she ever did a petty or a vain or a selfish action in her whole life.

APOSTOLIC BLOWS AND KNOX

The assumption now generally made that every man's religious opinions are deserving of respect has already borne melancholy fruit. There is, for example, the mincing tone we tend to adopt when speaking of one another's souls; and again, the common sight of two grown men discussing their religion and being very intense and unutterable about it. No religion has ever produced a creature as reverent as the reverent agnostic. This sort of thing ends in a snuffle, and snuffling is the ruin of religion.

But *are* a man's religious opinions deserving of respect? The man is, certainly; but his religious opinions may or may not be. The result of a man's thinking on religion is no more necessarily deserving of respect than the result of his thinking in any other field. To pretend a respect for it that one does not feel is to treat the man as a child, whose efforts must be taken very seriously lest it burst into tears. In other words, to treat a man's religion with more respect than it deserves is to treat the man with less respect than *he* deserves.

In *Broadcast Minds,* Father Ronald Knox avoids this mistake. He is concerned with the religion and philosophy taught in England over the radio by such men as Bertrand Russell, Julian Huxley, H. G. Wells and Langdon Davies: because the same kind of thing is being broadcast in America, he includes an examination of H. L. Mencken. Because mushiness has broken out and is spreading rapidly, the book is of importance. On the principle just laid down—that respect for a man expresses itself in a certain freedom of handling—he treats his subjects with a respect that might almost be called exaggerated; with some of them, indeed—Huxley, for example, and Mencken—he carries his respect to the point of vivisection, so faithfully does he strive for a true evaluation of their religious opinions. This has led one reviewer to attack the whole book as mere controversy; which raises the question "when is controversy mere?"

Now in this sense there is no tradition of religious discussion. Most often, such discussion as we have known has been reducible to a Protestant saying that Alexander VI had four children, and a Catholic retorting that Henry VIII had six wives. Thus religious controversy has acquired a thoroughly bad name, and it is easy to realise how beautiful silence would sound by comparison. Silence, however, is what men never can maintain about religion; and the convention of "respect," brought in to protect us against controversy, has left us at the mercy of that reverent snuffle already noticed.

If thought on religion is to be saved, free discussion must come back; a whole province of the human mind cannot be ruled off from criticism. A man who does not want his religious opinions criticised should keep them to himself: to utter them is to offer them, and you cannot offer your views with a proviso that they are for admiration only.

Criticism, even strong criticism, of some other man's religion, is not necessarily bigotry; nor are the emotions of strength wrong or un-Christian, as the emotions of weakness are. In *Broadcast Minds*, Fr. Knox is angry when he discusses those who patronise Our Lord. But anger does not spoil discussion, though temper may and bitterness does—especially when it is allied with irrelevance. Laughter, of course, is allowable—that is, laughter that laughs:

the laughter a man laughs in his sleeve may be poisonous, and facetiousness is always very pitiful.

How then are we to differentiate discussion of religion, which is right and necessary, from mere controversialism and quarrelsomeness. It is difficult to set down precise rules easy to follow. The avoidance of irrelevance is plain and straightforward enough; but when we say anger may be right and temper wrong, how is a man in a temper to know the difference? No advice will enable a shrew to see that she is nagging, or a bigot that he is writing bigotry. They know no different, and you only puzzle them by trying to reason about it. The truth is that it is not a matter of rules at all, but of character. The first thing is not to *be* bigoted or shrewish; the second thing is to shake free of bad conventions in discussion, created by bigots and carried on, simply because they are conventions, by decent men. But the pressing need is that that fine thing religious discussion should not be left entirely to the bigots and the shrews, but should come more and more into the hands of men.

VITAL SCHOLASTICISM

There are two ways of acquiring a philosophy. One is to study an existing philosophical system, gain as profound an understanding of it as possible, and keep referring back to the universe of being to see if it bears out what philosophers have said. In this method, the object of study is the philosophical system, the universe being used, so to say, merely as a check-up. The other method is to study the universe, wrestle with it, fall into mental agony trying to solve the questions it raises, and then turn to the philosophers to find if perchance they can throw any light on the same questions.

The former is the usual method, the philosophy-without-tears method, and its curse is slickness. The universe peeps coyly up at the student from the pages of his textbook, having never thrust its perturbing presence through his front window. He has learned the answers before he has felt the questions, which robs the questions of all their terrors: also of all their meaning. This method produces excellent teachers of philosophy, but not philosophers.

The second method is only for the minority. And of those who try it, some suffer irreparably. For as the curse of the first method is slickness, so the danger of the second method is despair. But some emerge with their minds established in a view: and these, whether their view be a right one or an erroneous one, are philosophers. Their questions are their own. Their philosophy is the real reaction of their own mind to the universe which has been their mind's first love. The significance of Edward Watkin (as of Peter Wust in Germany) is that he has followed the second road.

Already in *The Bow in the Clouds* he had shown it; and *A Philosophy of Form* is his answer to the demand that he produce an explicit presentation of the philosophy implicit in the earlier book. He is indubitably a scholastic: but one who has weighed the opinions of many masters— of Plato, Augustine, Scotus Erigena, Anselm and Bonaventure, and not only of Aristotle, St. Albert and St. Thomas; of Descartes and every considerable modern philosopher.

Yet for all this range, the result is a genuine philosophy and not a patchwork. It is obviously impossible to analyse it. It is a philosophy of Form and thus is both speculative and practical; for "the entire fabric of knowledge and *consequently of action and production* is founded on contemplation," and "contemplation is an intuition of form." These statements obviously involve both a metaphysic and a theory of knowledge. The metaphysic is close enough to the classical Thomist, though with one or two brilliant contributions of his own; but the theory of knowledge is far more original—and deserves the closest consideration. It is a development so daring as to look like a revolution.

His philosophy, once stated, is applied to every range of human experience. The chapters on art, on sociology and on mystical union with God are, if not of greater value than the rest, at least of greater appositeness.

DAWSON AND THE CRISIS

The worst part of philosophy, says Father Vincent McNabb, is the history of philosophy; and the best part of history is the philosophy of history. The ordinary fact-grubbing historian is merely the drudge of the philosophic historian, in whose hands we all are; for he makes revolutions. He interprets history as class-struggle, and you have Bolshevik Russia. He interprets history as Aryan, and you have Hitler's Germany. The significance of Christopher Dawson is that he is a (or perhaps the) Catholic philosopher of history. And because he is that, he is more. For a philosophy of history is not enough: we need a theology of history. Unless we know what history began in—a catastrophe that left a permanent mark on man's nature—and what it is to end in, and whether or not it is purposive, our philosophy of it must be only a guess; and these three things we can know only by revelation from God.

What revelation teaches, history confirms. Without revelation, one could not have known the interpretation; once one has the interpretation, it fits the facts. No other does. If his book, *Religion and the Modern State,* contained nothing but the chapters comparing the Marxian interpretation of history with the Catholic, it would be essential for the understanding of the principal modern problems. For it is as a historian relying on the facts of history and not as a theologian quoting the word of God that Dawson shows the aptness of the one interpretation and the ineptness of the other. He is unique among Catholic critics of Marx because Marx as a human problem fascinates him. The Messianic hope which was in him as in every Jew—"burnt into the very fibre of his being by centuries of thwarted social impulse in the squalid Ghettos of Germany and Poland"—entered into an impossible alliance with his materialist philosophy and wrecked it; and though he did not realise the wreck, it has introduced a contradiction in his system which is still present in Bolshevism.

For our present discontents, the important thing (so history teaches) is that the remedy is to be sought primarily in a change of spirit and only subsequently in a change of social mechanism. But the change of mechanism, if secondary, will have to come. The Catholic knows that there is no abiding city here below, and no perfection for man upon earth. But that does not mean that the social machine is to be abandoned, as not worth repair. Dawson's final chapters are concerned with the principle that must be followed in the repairing, principles all the more urgent because the competing social systems—Communism as in Russia, Hitlerism as in Germany, Capitalism and Liberal Democracy in the Western Countries—are all moving to the same goal, which is "the mechanisation of human life and the complete subordination of the individual to the state and to the economic process." In face of that threat, preferences will not help, nor instincts. Only principles can save us. Here are principles.

A SECOND THOUGHT ON
RELIGION AND THE MODERN STATE

Truly I do not know of another book so precisely apt to this moment as Dawson's *Religion and the Modern State*. To call it the political testament of present-day Christianity would be too vague, yet one feels that some such resounding title is needed to convey its importance. In structure it is an examination of the Dictatorships, Fascism and Communism and the Economic Interpretation of History, followed by a statement of the Catholic view of history (as the action of God in human affairs) and sociology. It does not offer a program: it does not solve present problems. It builds the mind with which Christians can set about solving them. What is in question is not a handful of simple rules-of-thumb, but a really profound re-making of the mind. Only from minds thus re-made can practical solutions of any value proceed.

In an essay in *Ways and Crossways* Paul Claudel states the essential problem: all governments sooner or later come to a certain "dull irritation" with Christianity because Christians may be perfectly loyal yet *cannot* take them as seriously as they take themselves. Christians cannot see them as really sovereign but only as overseers of material and therefore perishable interests: "the neighborhood of Eternity is dangerous for the perishable," and the Christian lives in the neighborhood of eternity.

But this surprisingly does not mean that the Christian is indifferent to the governance of earthly things; on the contrary even while seeing that they are secondary, he also sees that they are God's and that he will have to give to

God an exact account of them: "There are many more
people than you think who by natural laziness would be
prepared to forsake anything you like but precisely because nothing belongs to him, the Christian can yield
nothing." Thus there is for the Catholic no question of
oriental submission: but a tenacious stand in defence of
things which he knows to be secondary and perishable, but
entrusted to his stewardship by God.

Thus Claudel states the two elements; and in his own
life lives them, for he who thus shows the "provisoriness"
of all governments existent or even thinkable here below,
has been one of France's greatest ambassadors. It is of this
double problem that Dawson treats in *Religion and the
Modern State*: unless the Christian sees both sides of it,
he will but add one more muddling finger to a pie already
over-fingered. Once he has seen and fully meditated both
sides, he may produce something more valuable. It is
thus that the book is being widely used. Christian men of
the most differing outlooks attest its value. Thus the
Anglican Bishop of Chichester would have all his candi-
dates for ordination study it. In the last presidential election campaign, I met a man high in Roosevelt's support and another man a leader in the anti-Roosevelt camp
both speaking of the book, almost with awe; and so also
spoke of it a Minister Plenipotentiary of one of the South
American Republics. The *Catholic Worker* approves of it,
and all recent Catholic speakers and writers against Communism are obviously soaked in it.

For in this book is the common ground from which all
Catholic social thinkers, wherever they may ultimately
emerge, *must* start.

ORCHARD'S BAY

There are lovelier flowers in books than ever bloomed in any garden. No gardener will ever grow flowers to equal Shelley's violets, Herrick's daffodils, Ophelia's rosemary, the daisies that Jean Froissart loved above all flowers, and the rose that budded for Ronsard and his Mignonne. Most of us are but pallid flower-lovers in a garden, whereas a flower in a poem can thrill us to the heart's core. We admire flowers in a garden, but simply as ornamental vegetables: they are beautiful, but only in poetry do they become magical. This is true of most natural loveliness. The wind could blow across a bank of wild thyme for weeks and we would notice vaguely that there was a nice smell: but let a poet mention the same wind and we are lifted from that moment into a reality for which there are no words. The poet can say "My heart leaps up when I behold a rainbow in the sky"; whereas mine leaps up when I behold a rainbow in a book—and it's no bookish rainbow, either; it's the real rainbow and I'm really beholding it because the poet has beheld it first.

But let us return to gardens, and to one particular garden, Alfred Noyes's. It is one of the loveliest in England and it illustrates my point perfectly. I have strolled through it a dozen times and have loved it, without passion. Now Alfred Noyes has written a book about it—*Orchard's Bay* (mainly in prose but scattered among the prose some forty poems, the largest body of lyrics published by Alfred Noyes since 1924)—immortalizing the garden, as I half suspect; and I see the flowers in the book as I never saw them in the garden. I see them in the book as the poet sees them in themselves. For me (and most readers will be in the same case) the book is more truly the garden than the garden is.

But Alfred Noyes is not merely painting a picture of a garden. What he sees there sets his mind moving and there is nothing you cannot be set to thinking of in a garden if you have the right kind of mind. As he puts it: "Almost everything about a garden has a curious symbolism of its own. It hints at hidden meanings, as though one were walking in a lovely parable. It stands apart from wild Nature; and, from Eden to Gethsemane, its beauty has been interwoven with the deepest thoughts of man concerning his origin and end."

Anything that can happen between man's origin and his end is liable to turn up in these pages, and by the oddest associations—as when laurel sets the author thinking about witch-burning and from the star-white blossoms of the laurustinus he proceeds by two removes to the vicar's nose. You would never guess those two removes.

MARRIAGE

Most of the present-day talk on marriage is being done by the heart. Which, you say, is as it should be. Perhaps so: but in that case the heart should speak frankly *as* the heart, the final arbiter as to what we like. Whereas it is masquerading as the *head* and claiming to decide what is right. True it is that we like all things and desire them *as good*, but not necessarily are they good for us nor rightly ranged in their order. It is for head to say what marriage is: and heart may then proceed to say either "I like it" or "I don't like it." If it follows up "I don't like it" with "I won't have it," heart may be acting disastrously but not nonsensically: for it is acting *as* heart, which is what it is.

Consider now, with quiet heart and active head (which is one of the scholastic definitions of heaven), the situation of the human race. One of its prime duties is to get itself carried on—to get new children born and nurtured to maturity. It is not everyone's job, but it is the race's job.* But this carrying on of the race—a difficult and delicate matter demanding a certain repose and a certain stability—is made dependent upon sex-appetite, the stormiest and unruliest of all human appetites. The problem then is how the stormy and unruly thing is to be made to subserve the thing that demands permanence and stability. The answer is marriage. It takes hold of sex, orders, controls and directs it: and the new generations of men are born and reared. Nor is sex diminished but immensely enriched—for it is concentrated and not dissipated, drawing strength from life as a totality instead of being isolated in an autonomy

* Cf. Christopher Dawson's essay "Christianity and Sex" in his *Enquiries*.

for which it is not big enough. Any serious consideration of marriage must begin with its place between sex and the future of the race, as it adapts the one for the use of the other.

This is the excuse for purely theoretical, head-y books on marriage. A reader of *Nullity of Marriage* (by me) complained that it reduced marriage to a well-articulated set of dry bones. The statement is true, but the complaint is unjustified. The question is: Can these dry bones live? and that is for love and courage and virility to answer. But the bones are to be made to *live*, not simply pulled asunder or shaped into more pleasing outlines, or utterly ignored. Helen of Troy was, it would seem, beautiful. I doubt if her skeleton was. Yet the one was totally supported by the other. Christian marriage is not a skeleton, but it has one. And any attempt to remould it must be based upon what the skeleton will allow.

Anyhow, whether the complaint was or was not justified in the instance of *Nullity of Marriage*, it will not be made about Fr. Joyce's monumental *Christian Marriage*. It is concerned in part with the nature of marriage as a natural relationship and as a sacrament: but its main concern is historical: and its theme might almost be described as the story of how the head has steadily maintained the right view of marriage against the impulses and persuasions of the heart. Face to face with the civil law of old Rome, the customary law of the Germanic peoples, the self-will of mediæval rulers, the naturalistic arguments of the moderns, the Church has maintained her position that marriage has certain properties by the law of God, with which neither the Church nor anyone else can interfere; within this framework, the Church herself makes further regulations, which as they are her own, she can alter at will. All this Fr. Joyce shows in great detail, together with the efforts made to solve similar problems by the Greek Orthodox Churches. Apart from its interest for scholars, his book should help towards the reconciliation of heart and head which is needed if the institution of marriage as we know it, and as it is part of the structure of our civilisation, is to survive.

REVERIE ON A LAWYER

The Tudor period is notable for dubious characters—people, that is, who used to be thought extremely good and are now under a suspicion that hardens steadily. Once Queen Bess was Good and Mary was Bloody. But now, which of them was which?

From end to end of that period there is one man upon whose greatness of mind and character there is no dispute at all. Only one. Thomas More. "Indeed," says Professor Chambers,* "the love of Sir Thomas More is one which joins together many and diverse spirits, as does the love of the mountains, or of St. Francis of Assisi." Henry VIII. (father of the Good one and the Bloody one, whichever was which), who in any case would not have cared for mountains or even for St. Francis, beheaded him.

Now this was no great distinction. To the Tudor axe all heads were alike—Anne Boleyn, More, Fisher, Katherine Howard and a hundred or so others—a very diverse list with only the axe for a unifying principle. But in this case of More, the headsman set a fashion. Subsequent historians have followed slavishly his cleaving asunder of a unity. For in general it seems fair to say that the non-Catholic writer has concentrated on the head and the Catholic writer has neglected the head. A head without a man is as defective as a man without a head. It remained for someone to see the whole man, head and all, and Daniel Sargent, it would seem, has done it.

Tradition, by the way, did better than the serious historian in this matter. It kept steadily on with a handful of

* In *The Fame of Blessed Thomas More.*

98

jokes, which were formed in the head but rooted in the whole character: to their making the lawyer, the husband, the scholar, the sage and the saint all contributed. One might write for weeks about those jokes. They came out of a hair-shirt, for instance, which may account for a certain difference of quality between More's jokes and the jokes of—say—Will Rogers or *Punch*. Jokes that fight their way to the outer air through a hair-shirt are likely to have a high-survival value—like the babies of Sparta. Again, the jokes were a grave charge against him in the Puritan mouths of the next century or so—particularly that he should have joked on the way up the scaffold steps. It was held, apparently, as a sign of frivolity. I suggest that some-one might write a thesis on the absence of jokes in Foxe's *Book of Martyrs*. Not one of these men died laughing.

Note also that they were good jokes—almost the first good jokes in history made by a notable man. Before the sixteenth century, did any notable man say anything which to a modern seems to be even remotely funny? Save of course in the unconscious funniness of such things as the "above suspicion" of Cæsar's wife, or Nero's "Qualis artifex pereo."

Anyhow, between joke and earnest, the man is worth meeting: and in Sargent's *Thomas More* it is the man you meet.

LIFE IN THE CITY

The relation between Arnold Lunn's *Within That City* and his earlier *Now I See* is thus stated by himself: "Those who have done what they could to justify at the bar of reason the credo with which they enter the Church may perhaps be forgiven if some years later they confess not only their faith but their love."

It would not be too extravagant to say that Arnold Lunn made a forced marriage with the Church (his own intellect holding the gun, but his heart stone cold) and fell in love with her afterwards. *Now I See* was the account of an intellectual conviction: from Chaos he was coming into the City: he knew Chaos for what it was, but his heart yearned back towards the freedom and the beauty he had known in it: for if he knew that Truth was in the City, he had yet to learn that "the visible beauty of the hills which I had loved as a boy was linked by a kind of necessary connection with the invisible beauty which I had discovered as a man."

He hits off the reality of life in the Church in small things—as in the phrase about "vanity bags which are left in the pews what time their possessors are confessing to vanity in the Confessional"; and he hits it off in great. Consider what he has to say of Doubts—"In the before-conversion period, when doubts came, I wondered whether they would ever go: now I only ask myself when they will go. . . . There are still unsolved difficulties, to which I have yet to find a satisfactory answer, but I have discovered a key which unlocks nine locks out of ten, and it is not the fault of the key but of my wrist that the tenth lock proves rather sticky."

"Credo means I believe: it does not mean I behave." Thus he crystallizes an admirable discussion of the Church as the home of sinners.

"The Church is, indeed, the natural home of those who pray with difficulty." This is his summary of a couple of chapters on Prayer which are possibly unique in spiritual literature. For they are not the writing of a priest telling men how they should pray, but of a layman describing how he (like millions of other not particularly spiritual Catholics) does pray.

For one who would make a mere visit of inspection to the City, this book is indispensable: and even the Oldest Inhabitant will know his City the better for it.

DOGMA EXCITES CLAUDEL

The mysteries of religion may be a mere form of words in the mind. Apart from that placid extreme, they will be either a light to the mind or a trial to the mind. The alternative is presenting itself with growing insistence: in the religious life of the individual, its importance is capital. The great revealed dogmas, it is obvious, were meant to give light—light being what revelation is for. It is equally obvious, as has already been noted, that for many they are a burden greater than the mind can bear. What makes the difference?

The answer is almost too simple. Mysteries are rather like nettles: if they are not grasped firmly they are a powerful irritant: for their first face is contradiction. But to the mind which is prepared to turn its full gaze upon them, they are a powerful illuminant. For to the mind which thus searches into them, while the mystery remains no less, the contradiction disappears. The mind, then, is not baffled by contradiction, which is its mortal enemy, but strengthened by the realised presence of truths mightier than itself. But to have them dangling in the mind, half seen, glimpsed and then blacked out, to the accompaniment of a guilty feeling that one ought not to be looking at them at all, is the sort of maddening experience that finally proves altogether intolerable.

Mysteries, then, are an invitation to thought: and while their content is infinite and never to be exhausted, the mind can steadily draw out of them truth, which is its proper food.

Because Paul Claudel has fully grasped this, his *Ways*

and Crossways will be for many a revelation. In each essay he faces some mystery of the faith, and sets out with admirable lucidity what he finds in it. The doctrine of Transubstantiation, for instance, enriches the mind with a totally new view of matter: the doctrine of Eternal Punishment is a mine of truth about the nature of the human soul—and particularly of the human will. A study of the mysteries transfigures the whole world. And between the state of mind in which the mysteries are an obstacle in the way of religion and the state in which religion would be seen as barren and empty without them, there is a development beyond all measure.

ESSENCE OF CHESTERTON

The Well and the Shallows contains priceless material for Chesterton's biography, none of it more revealing than the essay *Mary and the Convert*. There is not a word of that essay which the Chesterton lover can afford to miss; but there is one passage illuminating above the rest. Speaking of his own Protestant boyhood, he says:

I can distinctly remember reciting the lines of the "Hymn To Proserpine," out of pleasure in their roll and resonance; but deliberately directing them away from Swinburne's intention, and supposing them addressed to the new Christian Queen of life, rather than to the fallen Pagan queen of death.

> *But I turn to her still: having seen she shall*
> *surely abide in the end;*
> *Goddess and maiden and queen, be near me*
> *now and befriend.*

And I had obscurely, from that time onwards, the very vague but slowly clarifying idea of defending all that Constantine had set up, just as Swinburne's Pagan had defended all he had thrown down.

It is the characteristic of Chesterton, as of that vastly different man Belloc, that the names of Constantine and Our Lady should thus be linked. Superficially the two names might seem to stand at opposite poles of Catholicism, on the one hand organization crushing the spirit, on the other religion at its tenderest. It is this single devotion to two seeming incompatibles that gives these two men their special glamour—for glamorous they are, living and known to us yet already legendary, as no other of their contemporaries in the Church or out of it.

The man who in our day has the notion of "defending all that Constantine had set up," is taking on a bigger job than anyone since Constantine; saving it, indeed, may be more difficult than setting it up. For those who would seduce us from it come strengthened with its own rich gifts; and the rival city (not yet built but that is a detail) is presented by its enterprising realtors as embodying all the best features of the dear old City which our ancestors thought was of God but which we have outgrown. *The Well and the Shallows* is really a survey by Chesterton of the roads that lead away into the wilderness. For such a survey he had the perfect eye. It is surprising how under his mild gaze (for no satirist ever had a milder eye) what looked like a firm straight road begins—as it were—to shift guiltily and ends as a wavering absurdity, leading nowhere, supporting no one. To misuse his own phrase—

> *And so the roads they twist and squirm*
> *If I may be allowed the term.*

A thing that has once been seen through the eye of Chesterton seldom returns to the shape men once thought it had.

UNDER THE SKIN

"Philosophy," says Maritain, "is competent to judge every other human science"; scientists cannot escape the judgment of philosophy even when they remain within their science, still less when they leave their test-tubes or statistical charts and do a little philosophising on their own account. The trouble is that the philosopher who should be acting the Judge is too busy acting the Advocate, and what should be a judicial inquiry becomes a battle. It seems to us the special excellence of Edward Watkin's *Men and Tendencies* that it gives us rather the sense of a judge summing up than of a litigant letting himself go in the happy absence of his opponent.

One result of this is that he sees the hidden points of agreement in men he disagrees with. In the essay on H. G. Wells, he pays continued tribute to the power of Wells's vision and the rightness of his instinct: "Wells is like a man attempting to escape from a dark room. He glimpses a ray of light from outside. But he cannot find the door beneath which it enters and through which he might escape. . . . He can but cast wistful glances in the direction of the light—the immortal and unlimited Life for which man is made. But he cannot move towards it. For he is sure there is nothing higher than man and his natural human life."

So, likewise, of Galsworthy. Finding one of Galsworthy's characters saying, "You want something beyond emotion, I think, you want to grasp infinite invention going on in infinite stillness. Perpetual motion and perpetual quiet at the same time"—Watkin comments: "How close this description approaches the religious experience of God. An infinite energy which yet is an infinite stillness. Though he is unable to state it correctly, he is evidently striving to express the intuition for which Aristotle found a more adequate formula."

And of Havelock Ellis: "He has been a pioneer in the scientific study of sex and that study has led him to describe at length the most unpleasant and bizarre perversions of the sexual instinct. But these studies have not led him, as sexual preoccupation has led Freud, to interpret the whole of human life in terms of sex. Nor have they made him cynical. He is first and foremost an artist and a religious man—not however a religious believer. He stands, or rather kneels, in the outer court of the temple looking through the open door into the sanctuary where God is worshipped. But he does not enter."

In Aldous Huxley he finds little ground of agreement; in J. B. S. Haldane more. To Santayana he pays a glowing tribute: "It may be questioned whether, since Plato, there has been such a combination of the philosopher and the artist"; but of his philosophy he can only say, "The best in this kind are but shadows."

But it is in the long essay on the philosophy of Karl Marx that Watkin is at his most perfectly poised and the book at its highest value. In one sentence is the savour of the whole: "If the anti-Semitic prejudice of the Nazis and their English disciples charges the Jews with Bolshevism because Marx was a Jew, it must be replied that the only Jewish constituent of Marxism, the specific contribution of Marx *the Jew,* is its noblest feature—the ideal of an earthly order of social justice and peace. The materialism, the evolutionism and the dialectic on the other hand can boast of the purest Aryan ancestry."

FORMULA FOR FEENEY

In an early announcement of Father Feeney's new book *You'd Better Come Quietly,* we said that the author was as Catholic as Thomas Aquinas and as American as Mark Twain, with a strong streak of both in him. Now we always feel alarmed when people challenge us—as they often do—to defend the very letter of some statement made in an advertisement, for advertisements are written in rags and tatters of time snatched between the more solid jobs of publishing and cannot in the nature of the case represent the most finished expression of our ripest thought. But, as to this formula about Father Feeney, the more we look at it the better we like it. We shall probably never make another epigram as long as we live, but we'll go to the stake for the accuracy of this one.

Take the Mark Twain part. Father Feeney is a great humorist, though one almost apologizes for the use of a word which conjures up a picture of what may be called the Rotary-luncheon or Communion-breakfast style of speaker, who tells a stream of funny stories invented by someone else and so lives on other men's laughs. Forget these base men when you think of Father Feeney's humor. It is his own; it is not a succession of stories with a point, but a rich handling of life to find the funniness there is in it; and it is universal. I once saw two Jewish brokers from Wall Street chuckling over *Fish on Friday;* for you do not need to be a Catholic to appreciate him (though there are nuances that only a Catholic can get); you do not even need to be an American (say I in a strong Australian accent). In this present book turn to the sketch called

The Problem Mind. It is about Alps and Azores and Asparagus. It will show you what I mean.

Turn now to the other end of the formula, and note that in speaking of the Aquinas streak in him we have in mind the *Adoro te devote* and the *Lauda Sion* rather than the *Summa Theologica*. For Father Feeney dogma is not only true; it is breathlessly exciting. That is his special vocation—to make his readers feel the thrill.* The word "Gospel" means "Good news"; for the majority of us, it is still good but it is no longer news: our nerves are tired from too many sensations: we have grown numb and no longer react to the excitement of revealed truth. For that disease he is the perfect doctor. Plenty of writers can teach us lucidly what the doctrines are; he makes them matter to us personally.

In *You'd Better Come Quietly,* the title sketch, Father Feeney simply treats of the ladder of creation—inorganic matter, plant, animal, man: then far beyond the human race—nine unimaginable steps beyond it, the nine choirs of angels: and then, beyond the loftiest angel, a member of that human race we had left so far down the ladder—a girl who had a baby in Bethlehem. There is nothing in all this that we did not know. Yet as we read on, we remember confusedly a scriptural phrase about the morning stars shouting for joy and we feel like joining in the shouting.

I have deliberately made no mention of the crown of the book, the tour de force called *"Explaining the Trinity to Thomas Butler."* Anyone who has ever had so much as a lunch-table conversation with Father Feeney must have felt that there is far more in him than he ever managed to get down on paper; but in this note on the Trinity one stops feeling it.

* You may remember that something similar was said about Dr. Leen. In these two writers, you can study two ways of being thrilled.

SO WHAT?

Almost all street-corner speakers for Catholicism have had the same experience with the job of proving God's existence. They give the crowd St. Thomas's five proofs, together with certain superior home-made proofs of their own, and the effect is always the same. One constructs a perfect chain of evidence, displays it to the crowd with perfect cogency; but just when they should say "God exists" and fall on their knees, they say "So What?" and turn on their heels. They do not dispute the validity of the argument that there is a God; but they do not see how it matters to them whether there is or not. One might as well be proving that the sum of the angles of a triangle is two right angles; no one in the crowd would dispute it— save by chance some lunatic who has had a private revelation to the effect that triangles ought to have four sides. No one would dispute it. And no one would care.

What has impeded our apologists in the past has been that people have not bothered to say "So What?" *to them*, and the apologists therefore have redoubled their efforts to prove that God exists without realising that until men see the value of a truth for themselves, they will not bother themselves to accept it. The great quality of Father Martindale, most famous of English priests, is that people do say to him whatever is in their minds. (There is the incident of the workman sitting opposite him in the train. "Parsons is bloody," said the workman—bloody being a curse-word of some potency in England, a word no minister of the Gospel is supposed even to know the existence of. "There's bloodier," said Fr. Martindale. "Well, I'm damned," said the workman. "Not yet," said Fr. Martindale.) Therefore he has heard people say "So What?" And in the book *Does God Matter For Me?* he answers the question. He realizes that in doing so, he is thrusting into recesses of the soul that the average Englishman—whose difference from the average American seems to us less each year—would die rather than expose to public gaze. Thus he writes:

"I remember an unknown fellow-traveller leaning across in a railway carriage, putting a damp hand on my knee, and earnestly asking: 'May I inquire, sir, what are your Main Views?' It was obvious that the other passengers felt that this was a positive indecency and very nearly blushed, and even I felt inclined to tell him to go to blazes. Why, thought I, should I be obliged to exhibit the very things that I, a sheepish Englishman, prefer to keep so wrapped up that I hardly ever look at them myself?"

If we are right in thinking that the importance (rather than the fact) of God's existence is the principal question of modern apologetics, then this book is vital. For the indifferentist. For the Catholic. Above all there is in Fr. Martindale none of that glibness which destroys the confidence of the modern young more surely than any other fault.

DOSTOIEVSKY

If Communism overwhelms us, it will be because we have not troubled to understand it. To regard it as a question of how property shall be distributed or which class shall govern the State is like regarding an explosion of dynamite as something that might blow your hat off. Holding your hat on is not a sufficient precaution against dynamite, and stating the arguments for private property is derisory as a way of meeting Communism. It is a religious question, a question of God and immortality and the destructive possibilities of the human will. It cannot be met with anything but God. But we cannot use God as a convenience—something to batter Communism with. There is too much blasphemy of that sort already. We can use God only on condition of letting God use us. And this might be rather more upsetting to our habits than Communism.

It is a special value of Dostoievsky, and of Nicholas Berdyaev who has just written a book on him, that both men see this fully. "Generally speaking," writes Berdyaev, "the conflict between revolutionaries and counter-revolutionaries is a superficial affair, *an opposition of interests.* . . . Socialism can be fought successfully only on the spiritual plane, as Dostoievsky fought it, and not on the ground of the bourgeois interests against which it maintains its claims." In this matter the great Russian novelist saw exactly right. So much so that he did in the sixties prophesy the whole Marxian development: the Bolshevik revolution has been, almost in detail, "according to Dostoievsky."

But his value for our world in that matter is only part of his general value. Consider his definition of reality—"the relations of man with God and with Satan." His novels all have this as their governing idea. He sees the life of society as a thin crust with "the impassioned and tumultuous dynamism of human nature" gradually working up to explosion underneath. It is this secret part of human nature that is his concern, and he seeks it in man's unconsciousness, folly, insanity, criminality—for here, the destructive possibilities that are in *every* soul, since the sin of the first man, have thrust themselves above the surface and can be studied.

Dostoievsky, of course, is not to be read without reserves. He was a Russian, and the Russian spirit tends to extremes —to atheism and nihilism at the one end, to an ecstatic and apocalyptic religion at the other. He did not fully grasp Catholicism, and this is important not because it led him to attack it (which he did), but because many things were left dark to him which Catholicism might have illumined—he could not for instance see the love of man and woman as anything but distortion and destruction because he had never grasped the Catholic teaching of "the fusion of two souls into one, the making of two bodies one." But he saw two things with absolute clarity: that life was a thing of tragic seriousness, and that only in Christ can the human tragedy be resolved. How these two truths energise in Dostoievsky's work, Berdyaev shows. But because Berdyaev is a genius in his own right, his book will be read as a commentary on life itself, even more significant than *The End of Our Time.*

BELLOC—POET

In the greatest statue there is nothing but stone; in the greatest poem, nothing but words. The rest is magic. Sometimes (as with Francis Thompson) you can analyze the magic—putting your finger on the glowing word or figure of speech that lifts you out of your chair. But with the greater it is plain magic: you not only cannot see how they do it: you cannot even see what they have done: you only know that for that instant they have lifted you into reality. That is what Belloc does: he does it in his prose: he does it more surely and continually in his poetry. Reading his *Sonnets and Verse* we have the experience time and again.

What is his special quality? In one epigram (not here quoted for its magic, by the way) he writes:

> *I'm tired of Love: I'm still more tired of Rhyme*
> *But Money gives me pleasure all the time.*

He calls this "Fatigue"; but whatever fatigue Belloc-the-man feels, Belloc-the-poet's fatigue is more vivid than another man's energy. Indeed it is this sense of enormous life even in his quietude that distinguishes him from all the forward looking poets of our day.

I am not so foolish as to try to "appreciate" Belloc's poetry. A symphony can be described only in the language of a symphony. If I were capable of saying what I feel as I read him, I should be a poet myself and the world would have one publisher fewer to cumber it. I could catalogue certain special notes of his excellence: as that even his mockery is poetry (a very exacting test this): that he does the shop-soiled themes of wine and roses as Horace might have done them had he loved the Trinity and God Incarnate and Our Lady: that his ballade refrains are complete poems in themselves—like "The devil didn't like them and they died." But nobody wants an inventory and what is wanted I cannot write: if I could not learn to write like Belloc, why was I ever taught to write at all?

Anyhow, that there may be something written worthy of him in this note, let us end with a stanza of one of his poems to Our Lady:

> *Steep are the seas and savaging and cold*
> *In broken waters terrible to try;*
> *And vast against the winter night the wold,*
> *And harbourless for any sail to lie.*
> *But you shall lead me to the light, and I*
> *Shall hymn you in a harbour story told,*
> *This is the faith that I have held and hold,*
> *And this is that in which I mean to die.*

GERTRUD VON LE FORT

To us who believe, this world should be a hair raising place. But it is surprising what immensities we can take in our stride without the missing of a heartbeat. Heaven, hell, and purgatory are unnervingly close—not one split second's journey from wherever someone happens to die, yet we are not unnerved. And here and now we are living in two worlds—of matter and spirit—an acrobatic feat which no other being in the universe is called upon to perform, and we perform it with a sangfroid which is the mark, not of a complex situation mastered, but of a situation whose complexity is not comprehended: as a blind man is not giddy on the edge of an abyss.

Gertrud von le Fort sees all these things. She is a Catholic novelist in the only sense which is sense. For Catholic means universal, and a Catholic novelist is one whose mise-en-scène is the universe—not that bit of it which lies immediately under his nose, which he sees in the daylight and trips over in the dark—but the whole of it with all its parts and all its inhabitants. The secular novelist sees what's visible. The Catholic novelist sees what's there. He may or may not bring God and the angels as characters into his story, but they are always *factors* in his story (just as a painter cannot paint the wind and cannot paint the air but would produce a poor landscape without them). This is not to say that the Catholic is the better novelist. He may lack genius or art or even ordinary talent, so that he merely potters about on his universal stage while the secular novelist works magic with the little bit of universe which is all he has. But if by chance the Catholic has genius, then his novel cannot but be revelation. Gertrud von le Fort has genius.

There is one mild touch of paradox about her: This Catholic writer with the French name is German precisely because her ancestors were Protestant. The Barons Lefort were French Protestants, forced to flee from France because of their religion. By way of Savoy, Switzerland and Russia, her branch of the family came finally to settle in Germany: and the Baroness herself now lives (or did before the war) in a charming old house at Baierbrunn near Munich, looking down on the valley of the Isar. Her education was of the most thorough. She studied history and philosophy at the universities of Heidelberg and Berlin. She worked under the great Protestant philosopher Ernst Troeltsch (whose thought had so profound an influence upon Christopher Dawson). After his death she edited and published his theological writings, and in the same year, 1925, she entered the Church.

The three novels already done into English—*The Veil of Veronica, The Song from the Scaffold* and *The Pope from the Ghetto*—are very fully representative. In them all, both worlds are present in full reality; time is real but subordinated to, and occasionally altogether eclipsed by, eternity. Most typical is the third of the group, *Pope from the Ghetto.* The earthly action is immensely dynamic: the background is the half century of struggle between Popes and Emperors on the question of Investitures, the advances on Rome of Henry IV and Henry V, and Henry V's seizure of the Imperial Crown. In the foreground is the Jewish family of Pierleone, mother and daughter Hebrew of the Hebrew, father and son Christians, the father returning to Judaism on his deathbed, the son persisting in a Christianity he does not believe and becoming Cardinal and anti-Pope. Because Gertrud von le Fort sees all worlds at once, every action has immeasurable consequences: even material nature is held organically in the pattern. Doom is in the air, but only because the human will acts as it acts. I have said that this book is most typical of her universal outlook: in it the real protagonists (though their reality does not destroy that of the individual characters) are the three earthly institutions with the most immediate contacts with the supernatural—the Church, Jewry and (since it was in ideal the Kingdom of God in the Temporal order as the Church in the Spiritual) the Holy Roman Empire. The splendour and the misery of Jewry have never been so shown in a novel by Jew or Christian; nor the splendour and misery of the Catholic.

SOCIAL SERVICE

The slogan of the moment being Social Service let us consider what motives drive men to devote themselves to it. One motive is dislike of disorder: H. G. Wells would reform the world because it is messy, it offends his sense of arrangement (note also Bernard Shaw, who wishes to abolish the working classes "and replace them by sensible people"—*sensible* people, heaven help us). But this is a fad, lacks warmth, and will pass. Another motive is a passion for interfering: Belloc has fixed the type forever in *The Servile State,* and Chesterton in his commentary on Leigh Hunt's hero:

> *Abou Ben Adhem may his tribe decrease*
> *By cautious birth control and die in peace.*

This also is a fad and will pass. A third is pity for suffering: and this is both a nobler thing and a more effective thing. But by itself it can do more harm even than the others: because there are worse things than suffering. And historically the relief of suffering has been due almost invariably to men who knew that it was not the worst thing—who in their own lives showed that it could be a very good thing.

St. Peter Claver was such a man, and it is as a challenge to our modern conceptions of social service that Arnold Lunn depicts him.* Faced with the hellish conditions of the slave ships and the slave port of Cartagena he preached to the slaves, not about their sufferings but about their sins; so that the poor wretches began to inflict voluntary

* In *A Saint in the Slave Trade.*

penances upon themselves. But he also preached to the
slave-owners about *their* sins. And a by-product of his
work was so great an improvement in the treatment of
slaves that they were better off in Spanish Cartagena in
1600 than in British Jamaica in 1800.

Now but for what I have called this by-product, no one
would waste a moment's thought on Claver and his method
—which was, in one word, *to suffer with the suffering*. But
since he succeeded; since, even by the most rigidly non-
supernatural standards, he achieved such an alleviation of
suffering as the modern humanitarian does not dream of
achieving, his method cannot be dismissed with a flick of
the fingers. Mr. Wells and Mr. Shaw (I imagine—I have no
private information) do not wear hair-shirts: but their results are negligible compared with his. Had the hair-shirt
something to do with it? He thought it had. And until we
can beat him by our own standards, we can hardly assert
that he did not know what he was about.

Thus Arnold Lunn ranges over a whole list of vexed
questions—the nature of happiness, the implications of
love of one's neighbour, the principles of asceticism, the
rights of the body, the Catholic attitude to slavery. But
ever and again he forgets the modern mind and its blind-
nesses in the excitement of contemplating the incredible
life of Claver himself.

THINKING ORGANICALLY

The word "organic" has become *the* key word. We recognize it in the enormous emphasis on the Church as the Mystical Body—not simply a divinely founded organization to which we can resort for grace and truth, but a divine organism *in* whose life we live. We may not so clearly recognize that the same word is becoming all-important in the social-political sphere. Not to be alive to the implications of society as an organism is to be helpless for the discussion of society's diseases and the possible restoration of society to health.

That is why Ross Hoffman is so valuable. The concept "organism" is part of the structure of his mind. It is not simply something he knows about and can at need apply in his social judgments. It is so much part of his mind that he cannot not-apply it. It is a permanent light in which he sees everything. In that light his new book, *The Organic State,* judges our existing societies. His criticism of Democracy, as it is actually practised here and now, is searching to the point of ferocity. He sees it as "a hideous scene of folly, egoism and corruption." And he sees it in danger of destruction *not* from such external enemies as Fascism and Communism but from the growth of barbarism and atheism within itself. The problem is how to save it.

"Some believe," he writes, "that there is nothing wrong with the mechanism but only with the men; that the evil conditions of today, of debt, bungling, cowardice, corruption and so forth result wholly from stupidity, bad morals and the lack of a real public spirit in voters and politicians."

He does not accept this view. It is the mechanism itself that is wrong—and the principal thing wrong with it is that it *is* a mechanism and not an organism. It is not simply that it produces Congressmen or Members of Parliament who cannot think for themselves.* It is that the representatives individually do not represent any vital element in society; and that the political framework is not rooted in the life of society but perched precariously on top of it.

No one need agree with Ross Hoffman's thought. But we hope no one will think it can be neglected. Too much of our political thinking is superficial, concerned with symptoms rather than the real roots of disease: as though one were to treat leprosy with lipstick. In this crisis of the world we must get closer to the depths of things for, as we are, we are in danger of drowning in our own shallowness.

* My own mind moves absently toward W. S. Gilbert's song:
>   *But still the notion of a lot*
>   *Of dull MP's in close proximity*
>   *Each thinking for himself is what*
>   *No man can bear with equanimity.*

AN ANIMAL WITH A MIND

Man is an animal, and the difference between him and the other animals is not always obvious. You remember the limerick—

> *There was an old man of Antigua*
> *Whose wife said one day, "What a pig you are."*
> *He answered "My queen,*
> *Is it manners you mean,*
> *Or do you refer to my figuar?"*

which stresses the difficulty. Neither in manners nor in appearance can we *rely* upon the difference between man and other animals being manifest. I have already quoted a song which in recognizing the difficulty points to an answer:

> *Father's in the pig-sty*
> *You can tell him by his hat.*

You can distinguish man in general from the animals not actually by his hat but by his head—when, that is, he is using his head, not when he is simply wearing it. Man is an animal with a mind. The more he uses the mind, the greater the difference. If he gets tired and stops using the mind, he automaticaly comes closer to the animal level. The drag in that direction is always present. One sees it in small things, like the nudist movement: for while you may argue whether nudism is a good thing or a bad thing, there is no doubt whatever that it is an animal thing: had Father (in the song above quoted) been a nudist, there would not even have been the hat to tell him by.

In big things the drag is more serious. Man by his mind

has a twofold field of action possessed by no other animal—religion and art. Neglect either and we drift cow-wards: with all that air of wisdom, the cow is actually concerned only with her patch of grazing, knows nothing of adoration or beauty: we can get horribly like her.

Of religion we speak on other pages; here consider art. For long enough the plain man has been convinced of his impotence to understand art, has indeed gloried in knowing nothing of it. Quite recently the radio has made millions of people conscious of one of the arts—music—and of a response in themselves they had never dreamed possible. But for the most part they have not grasped what has happened within them. They think simply that they have acquired a taste for music: and as to the other arts—above all poetry—they still feel that there is no contact for them: whereas the reality that has reached them in music is reaching out for them in the other arts and a not-too-difficult rectification of vision would enable them to see it.

It is the importance of Blanche Mary Kelly's book *The Sudden Rose* that it offers to the plainest man the key to this great part of his heritage as a man. One who reads it will find that poetry (and pictures and sculpture) can do for him what music has already begun to do. And if anyone has not already had the experience of poetry and the rest and sees no reason why he should, let him take the first occasion to study a cow grazing and then take a long steady look at himself.

PREFACE TO METAPHYSICS

No man in his senses would try to "condense" Jacques Maritain's *Preface to Metaphysics* into two of these pages. There would be no point in it. For either you are already interested in Metaphysics, in which case all you need is to be told that the book exists, or else you are not at present aware of any interest in Metaphysics, in which case what you want is some sort of Preface to the Preface, giving you some reason why you should bother about it. And this is what I shall try to provide.

Metaphysics is the study of Being. And as everything that exists or can exist is a being, it is obviously necessary to be clear about that word if we are to understand anything at all.

That is not all. If you know all that "I am" means, then you know what God is. (If you have forgotten your grammar this may seem like a change of subject. We were talking about "being" a moment ago; and now we are talking of "I am." But "I am" is a part of the verb "to be." What a curse it is that the verb "to be" is irregular, so that half the time we are using it without noticing it. If only we could restore the dialectal forms "I be, you be, he be, we be, you be, they be" we should see a restoration of philosophy.)

To return to the importance of "I am." It is God's own name for Himself. "I am Who am" was His word about Himself to Moses. The phrase "The great I am" most of us know only as applied to some local politician: we have forgotten that it means "The great God." When Our Lord wished to assert his own divinity, he said "Before Abraham was made, I am." And in this sense there is a new light shining from some of his best known phrases—"*I am* the Way, the Truth and the Life." "*I am* the Resurrection and the Life."

Just as God calls himself "I am," so the Jews called him Jehovah, or Jahveh, which means "He is." When we have said "God is," we have said all that there is to say: only we do not know all we have said. Metaphysics is the record of man's progress in finding out, for it is the effort of the human mind to read what secrets are locked in the verb "to be."

For those who are already students of Metaphysics, I add that the book studies *being as such* [as distinct from (a) being as it is grasped by common sense, (b) being as it is studied by the Natural Sciences and (c) being as studied by Logic], and analyzes four of the first principles—Identity, Sufficient Reason, Finality and Causality.

And on the chance that you might like a sample, let me end with this: "It is not enough to employ the word 'being.' We must have the intuition, the intellectual perception of the inexhaustible and incomprehensible reality thus manifested as object. *It is this intuition that makes the metaphysician*.[1] . . . It is a sight whose content and implications no word of human speech can exhaust or adequately express and in which, in a moment of decisive emotion, the soul is in contact, a living, transpiercing and illuminating contact, with a reality which takes hold of it."

[1] Italics ours. Kant, says Maritain, never had it.

DON JOHN OF AUSTRIA

Don John of Austria needs some disentangling. In the mind of the general reader he is identified with Byron's Don Juan—and heaven knows, perhaps by now with Eric Linklater's: with contributions from Douglas Fairbanks for the lowbrow, and memories of a Mozart opera for the cultured. In the Index to the Catholic Encyclopedia he appears as a composite of himself and a later licentious person of the same name. That such a man should thus have become three parts submerged in a background of General Knowledge is a result of the process by which, in the English-speaking world, history has been so long treated as a branch of rhetoric. Patriotic rhetoric could obviously have no use for a sixteenth century Spanish Catholic who, beyond helping to save Europe from Mohammedan domination, did practically nothing at all.

Yet, obvious as this consideration is, it still remains a marvel that in any treatment of history he should have passed into obscurity. He was, as Margaret Yeo shows in the book she named after him, a man of tremendous action, and he had everything that is demanded of a hero of romantic fiction. He was the illegitimate son of the Emperor Charles V and Barbara Blomberg, a garrulous woman whose subsequent amorous adventures were relieved from total absurdity by nothing at all. Philip II acknowledged him as a brother and loved him as one. At 21 he had crushed the last great Moorish rebellion in Spain. At 24 he helped win the naval victory of Lepanto and ended the century-long threat of Turkish domination in Europe. He was sent by Philip II to the nearly impossible task of subduing the Netherlands. And there at 31 he died, in a ruined hut, in poverty and failure.

"The last knight of Europe," Chesterton calls him. With Don John dead, chivalry was at an end, and it was only left for Cervantes, who had served under him at Lepanto, to write *Don Quixote* as its funeral inscription. There was in chivalry an element of insubstantiality and melancholy which made it fitting that it should thus have produced its perfect specimen when it was already on its deathbed, should have produced the man who might have saved it when it was past saving. With his loyalty of motive, the consecration of his life to the overthrowing of God's enemies, the devotion to Our Lady, the almost ascetic rigour of his life, the reckless courage, the quick response to the challenge of the impossible, the final renunciation—he seems to have realised the ideal of chivalry as it never had in fact been realised in chivalry's heyday. His faults—ruthlessness while the battle was on, the two episodes of lawless love—were faults that the ideal allowed for. He came too late to save the order of knighthood, which fell as a legacy to the Walter Raleighs and Francis Bacons. He came just not too late to save Europe. Has Margaret Yeo come too late to save him, or must Douglas Fairbanks have the last word?

UNDER EUROPE'S SKIN

No matter where you live, it is horribly important to understand Europe. The trouble is that we are all getting our ideas of Europe from the Foreign Correspondents— either the little run-of-the-mill ones whom we read in our local papers or the de luxe ones who talk on the radio or write best-sellers. They really do know the last word about everything: but to quote Chesterton, "they don't know the first word about anything." They do not know enough of the past to tell us what anything means. What is worse, they see Europe as they might see Hollywood—in terms of the stars; of what the average man is thinking, above all of what the average man is like, they have not the faintest conception. But the present War is not a War of stars: even the Hitlers and the Stalins are only the symbols of mightier forces. And you will never learn what these forces are if you read only the Foreign Correspondents. Yet on one condition their books can be most illuminating—if you provide yourself with the background which they lack. And for such a purpose, Bernard Wall's *European Note-book* is admirable.

For Bernard Wall does not scurry over Europe. In normal times, he lives in Europe, sometimes in one country, sometimes in another; he lives as the people live, in a house, not a hotel; he reads the papers they read; he knows their past and all the influences that have shaped them. Above all he does not confuse one nation with another: he has the feel of the average man. The French middle-classes he tells us are "the most irate, the most discontented and the least truly polite. Politeness in the French street is the art of using courteous formulae in a menacing and suspi-

cious way. Life in Paris is a rosary of little quarrels, sar-
castic words."

The Italians? "Their temperament makes it difficult to
dragoon them and sixteen years of Fascism have not persuaded the Italian army to march in step; it is only recently that troops on the march have ceased calling out
endearments to all the pretty girls they pass, a practice difficult to stop as officers are perhaps more inclined to it than
men."

Spaniards? "You can't get into the average Spaniard's
head that Moors are foreigners."

And so with Poles, Germans, Jugo-Slavians—everybody.

He is just as realistic and concrete about ideological
trends. "It is difficult to understand the difference in spirit
between the political development of Modern Germany and
that of France unless we can grasp the contrast between
French rationalism and German romanticism."

This he says. This he proves. And proving it he makes
us see why the Frenchman thinks the German "barbaric"
and why the German thinks the Frenchman "sterile"; and
why so many attacks on Nazism leave the Nazi unmoved
because the very thing he is accused of he glories in: thus
if it is said that Nazism is the enemy of civilization, the
Nazi agrees—proudly. It is *very* important that we should
understand why or we shall never understand Nazism, and
it is impossible to understand what is happening in Europe
if we do not.

These things are picked out at random simply to show
the quality of the book. It is packed with them. Anyone
with the knack of writing and an eye for the louder colors
can take you for a gallop over the surface of Europe. Bernard Wall is one of the few who can take you under the
skin—and that is where the blood flows and the pulse beats.

THE NEW APOLOGETIC

It was still true, when Wilfrid Ward coined the phrase, that the Church was in a state of siege. It is hardly true now—at least so far as the theological field is concerned. The siege has quite suddenly been lifted from that quarter. But it lasted long enough for the siege-mentality to become pretty strongly ingrained. The essence of this mentality is an undue concentration on the city walls. The walls become an obsession; to them everything within the city must take second place. While the siege is on this is right: if the walls go, nothing stands. Yet in itself it is a reversal of the order of nature, and the life of the city must suffer. This was the Church's state for four hundred years. Against the unrelaxing attacks on the Church as an authoritative teacher, theologians had to concentrate on Papal Supremacy and Infallibility, the Marks of the Church, the proof of the Church's divine foundation. Naturally, therefore, the great body of revealed truth of which these other things are but the external support and framework had to receive less attention, and on that side there was a slowing down of development.

At any rate, the city was saved and the Church is free to concentrate once more on the truth of which she is the custodian rather than on the proof that she *is* its custodian. And this concentration on the content of the truths rather than on their demonstration has spread to Apologetic. Proof, as we have seen in an earlier essay, is of small value to people who are not greatly interested. The one thing that will arouse interest is the discovery that the truths matter. The New Apologetic therefore is concerned far more with showing what the dogmatic teaching of the

Church is and means than with proving that it is true. If only we can *show* the doctrines, they will tend of themselves to take possession of men's minds.

The books now being written within the Church are written in full awareness of this. But there is just the possibility that in this flood of new writing, many readers may not be able to find their bearings; in such a writer as Karl Adam certain doctrines are assumed as current coin which are by no means current coin. As publishers, we felt that a book was needed which should serve a double purpose. First, it should present the *synthesis* of Catholic doctrine as it exists in the mind of the great Catholic writers, so that readers and writers may start with the same general conspectus of Catholic teaching; Catholic doctrines not in a pile but in a pattern. Second, it should give the elements of those doctrines—particularly the Mystical Body and the Supernatural Life—without which the best Catholic writing of the day (to say nothing of Catholicism itself) can be only partially understood. We felt, I say, that such a book was necessary. Finally one of us tried to write it. The effort is called *A Map of Life*.

SEVEN MEN IN SEARCH OF THEIR AUTHOR

A child born into the world is as much a proof of the omnipotence of God as a dead man raised to life. Any natural happening proves God as much as any supernatural happening: the rising of the sun as much as the sun's standing still. Then why miracle? Because use dulls all edges; what we see too often we no longer see at all; and while logically the ordinary suffices to prove God's existence and presence, in the psychological order the extraordinary is needed to jerk us to attention.

This psychological rule, which is of universal application, explains Karl Pfleger's choice of subjects in *Wrestlers with Christ*. Christ is our sole possession here on earth; where this truth is unrealised, life is meaningless and must ultimately rush to destruction. Does the world realise it? Do we ourselves? Pfleger thinks not: "The world which professes Christianity is deeply enamoured of rest, habit and sleep. This was already plain on the Mount of Olives. But while the world endures, Christ is living even to the sweat of mortal agony."

This is a hard saying; and if any Christian feels that it is not true of himself—can say that there is no sleep in him while Christ is in agony—then this book is not for him. For the rest of us, the question is how we are to be forced back to vital realisation of a truth we know so well. One answer lies in these studies of the extraordinary: here are seven men—"poor, and in peril and unenlightened by the faith of the Church"; what they have in common is that they could not take Christ lightly. "Their agonising struggle for and with Christ is the positive and overwhelming proof of Christ's presence."

We may have got used to God-made-man, so that we can contemplate the shattering fact of the Incarnation with not so much as the stirring of a pulse; I doubt if anyone will take Léon Bloy lightly, and the agonised rending of nature that the acceptance of Our Lord caused him. Bloy, you say, was extreme; he was indeed, but there are two extremes in this matter and the contemplation of his may do something to stir us out of ours. Or, looking at Bloy and Péguy together, we may feel that they are just *too* extraordinary, so that we cannot relate our experiences to theirs at all; in that event, forget everything about them save the intensity of their realisation of Christ and see if our own saner Christianity leaves us altogether content. You may ask "What have Bloy and Péguy to teach me?"—to which one can only reply—"Perhaps nothing. But Péguy brought Ernest Psichari, Renan's grandson, to the Church; and Bloy brought Jacques Maritain."

But observe that these are not studies of exemplary Christians—not studies, so to speak, in success, but studies in struggle. Bloy and Chesterton and Soloviev wrestled with Christ and were vanquished by Him to their own success. Péguy was vanquished, but only in part—there remained a prodigious error and his story is a tragedy; Dostoievsky, emerged from his ghastly underworld, "clung to Christ with such burning of heart and mind *alike* as no other modern writer of his rank"—but it was hard for a mid-nineteenth-century Russian to find the Church which is Christ still living and working in the world; Berdyaev, the Russian Orthodox, still lives; and André Gide lives too, the man who had Our Lord and lost Him, and returned to Him and once more left Him, Gide in whom "the atmosphere of destruction and self-destruction which surrounds the typical man of to-day is focussed with an exceptional visibility."

It should be clear, by now, what Karl Pfleger's object is: to remind us, by these extraordinary examples, of the truth that everything depends on whether Christ is accepted. Therefore, even those who are not interested in the religious psychology of men of genius may treat his book as an alarm-clock. Its object is to wake us up, and it does not matter so much if our first waking action is to pitch the alarm-clock through the bedroom window.

THIS IS CONNEMARA

Anyone who sees Father Leo Richard Ward in his classroom at Notre Dame must see that he has the coolest eye imaginable. And a cool eye is the first thing you need if you are to write a book on Ireland. There are enough hot-eyed books already: the Irish laugh like anything at them. Very well. He had that! The girls he saw were girls, not colleens, and plain girls at that; the fiddlers he heard at country dances were very bad fiddlers. He was not on the look-out for magic: the bats that flutter in the Celtic twilight could not get into his belfry. So much, I say, you could see merely by looking at him. There is more of Iowa in his face than Ireland. What you do not see—unless you are especially skilled at looking—is that he has a genius for recreating the very reality of what he has seen.

His book, *God In An Irish Kitchen,* is more than a book about Ireland. It *is* the west of Ireland, and a marvellous place to be in, with no Mother Machree nonsense to cheapen its true pathos and no stage Irishry to parody its piercing humor. His power to make the reader see what he saw and feel what he felt is close to wizardry. By the time he gets you to the summit of Croagh Patrick you are as tired as he was; while he is doing the third day of the Lough Derg pilgrimage, your feet are aching and you are swearing that you'll never go again.

He starts in Galway—"a city that was cut to pieces long ago by a vigorous rough man named Cromwell"—with a visit to Kate Lannon, "a lean gull of a woman," and an encounter with "a pair of fat Australians, whom it would be difficult to think English, or Irish, or people at all."

From that moment we take every step of the way with him: and if there were nothing else to be said for the journey, we hear the English language used as a living thing with the sap in it, which is a way no one uses it but the Irish west of Dublin.

I say "if there were nothing else to be said for the journey." What else is there? The intimate kitcheny contact with a culture other than our own, spiritually closer to reality than our own, with different clearly-held values with which we may compare our own. For a vast section of us Catholics, too, this is the quarry from which we are hewn. There, but for the Great Famine or whatever other unpleasant circumstances dislodged our grandparents, we should still be. Dream of that!

RE-UNION

There is something about the divisions within Protestantism which so affects a Catholic's mind as to bar the way not only to understanding but even to the desire to understand. The whole thing looks to us like Bedlam and we leave it at that. But this Bedlam-look is deceptive. If any view is held by a considerable number of human beings it may be wrong, but it cannot be absurd. The phrase: "I can't make head or tail of it; it's all nonsense" refutes itself, as Chesterton noted. For if you can't make head or tail of it, how can you know that it is all nonsense? Further, if a man so states his case that it is on the face of it absurd, then be sure he has not done his view justice. This is what makes so much religious polemic valueless: you answer what the man says, but he knows it is not what he meant.

It is vital that Catholics should understand Protestantism; if they don't they will never make Protestants understand Catholicism. Protestants can only be converted by Catholics who can almost imagine themselves Protestants—that is who know why Protestants *are* Protestants. This is why *John Wesley* by the Franciscan Father Maximin Piette is so valuable a book for Catholics to read. For this Catholic priest quite literally loves John Wesley. As the book proceeds, the sense of Bedlam vanishes, because if the confusion of Protestantism is not lessened we are led to see how it came about and why the Protestant can live calmly in the midst of an apparent chaos which we feel would drive us mad. The first part of the book treats of the immediate consequences of the Reformation. The problem that faced the Reformers was to find some principle of order to replace the lost unity under authority. Luther turned to the protection of princes; Calvin to a strict Church organization; the Anabaptists to the sheerest individualism.

Two hundred years of this and England was filled with religions and almost empty of religion—plenty of sects and the mass of people in none of them. Then comes Wesley, and Father Piette's study is sympathetic and convincing. It is easy enough to make of his mother Susannah an attractive picture; less easy to win sympathy for his incredible father; easy again to show us Wesley himself studying the *Imitation of Christ*, coming to "conversion", facing the problem of his own vocation. But to weld into one clear structure all these things—and his missionary life with its endless journeying, and his forty thousand sermons, and the riots he had to face through, and the development of his own church—into one clear structure, is a triumph. The book, we repeat, should make for understanding; symbolic, therefore, is the fact that it has two prefaces, one by a Methodist divine, the other by a Catholic bishop.

THE LIFE-WORK OF KARL ADAM—I

With *The Son of God* Karl Adam completes a trilogy, a completion all the more telling because it should have come first. *The Spirit of Catholicism* is the book of Christ living in the Church. *Christ Our Brother* is Christ in His relation to the human race. In both books Christ in Himself is taken as known. Neither can yield much of its juice to readers who have only the vague and unspecified knowledge of Christ that the man of today can boast. The reader who returns to the two earlier books after reading *The Son of God* will find them almost totally new.

How vague is the modern idea of Christ can be seen whenever any publicist refers to Him. For the publicist is always wrong, and his public never knows it. (Consider Bernard Shaw: in the preface to *Androcles and the Lion* he proves by quotations respectively from Christ and St. Paul that the two differed in their views of marriage; and his argument would be a strong one only that *both* the quotations happen to be from St. Paul.) At any rate we have the modern man's tendency to identify Christ with his own better self; and we have the peculiar person's determination to picture Christ as the incarnation of his own peculiarity—vegetarianism, communism, teetotalism, spiritualism, pacifism, or what not; and the result is a figure very distressing to contemplate. A reading of the Gospels would blast that figure out of existence, but who nowadays will resort to so heroic an expedient as reading the Gospels?

The study of Christ Himself is the main theme of *The Son of God*. There is a framework. There are three

preliminary chapters in which are set out the problem as it
faces the man of today, the attitude of mind in which alone
profitably it can be approached, and the documentary and
other evidence at our disposal. There are concluding chapters on the Resurrection and a particularly powerful one
on the Atonement. But it is for the central theme that the
book will live.

Karl Adam approaches the study of Christ along the
oldest of all lines. To come to the study with a theory is
fatal, even if the theory is true—for the truth that Christ
is God almost stuns the mind that is unprepared for it.
What is needed is a pair of eyes, a pair of ears and a deep
reverence. Karl Adam divests himself of all but these three
things; and it will be noted that these were the only quali-
fications the Apostles had to begin with. Watch what He
does. Listen to what He says. There is no need to set the
fancy at work at its embroidering; artistry, imaginative
power are not needed, only close attention. All, and more
than all, that any mind can cope with is there in the Gospels. There will be few to whom this chapter of purely
external observation will not come as an absolute revelation; a reminder of Chesterton's words: "The grinding
power of the plain words of the Gospel story is like the
power of mill-stones; and those who can read them simply
enough will feel as if rocks had been rolled upon them."

The next step is the logical one. "What is told of Him
in the Gospels," says Adam, "is all unpremeditated, inimitable, uninventible, is so graven into His concrete,
work-a-day life, that only by starting with the living, working Jesus can we reach to His interior world." The interior
life comes next. Here again it is simply a case of looking
and listening.

By this time Karl Adam, and his reader, have traced the same mental course as the Apostles. Christ is seen and in a sense realised, as clearly human, and yet clearly superhuman. The mind—our mind like the mind of the Apostles—overwhelmed with what it has seen, reaches out for an explanation, half grasps at the true one, yet dares not hold it firmly because of its very magnitude, realises that only from Christ Himself can the answer come. He must provide the key to His own riddle. In the chapter, "The Self-Revelation of Jesus," we have the dogma of the Incarnation; and the enquiry has reached its term. Christ is God-made-man.

Karl Adam does not make the mistake of thinking this truth easy to believe. "A man who at this point, when confronted with the paradox of God the all-perfect, all-holy, eternal, becoming a man, a carpenter, a Jew haled before the court and crucified, shrinks away, can go no further, and breaks down, may be actually less remote from a living piety than one who coolly accepts all this and glibly repeats his *Credo*. But in the question of all questions has man, for all his faith and his conception of God, really the last word? Is not God greater than man's conception of God? In the infinite possibilities of God all conceivable possibilities are included, even the possibility of a Bethlehem and a Golgotha. We cannot ignore Jesus. He is a possibility of God's."

THE LIFE-WORK OF KARL ADAM—II

Karl Adam is a man of two doctrines—the Incarnation and the Mystical Body—and these come simply to one fact. His whole mind is concentrated on Christ. His theology of course is not of his own invention: yet there must be something special to the man to account for his phenomenal influence on the religious mind of Germany and England.

One such special quality—it may be the dominant one—is his treatment of mystery in religion. Every mystery resolves itself into two statements which appear to be irreconcilable. By faith in God's word we accept both, assured that there is a reconciliation even if we cannot at present see it. But though we accept both, in practice there is a tendency to select one as the primary one, the effective one, the solidly established one: the other we regard as the problem, the one that needs to be reconciled, and pending reconciliation, to be kept in the background and not dwelt on too much. Thus in the Trinity, it is simplest to dwell on the oneness of God and glide lightly over the threefold personality. (The Greeks, it would seem, dwell rather on the three-fold personality and treat the oneness as the mystery requiring solution.) Now this tendency does, it is true, make for a quiet life: if, of two apparently irreconcilable statements, one is accepted and stressed and the other accepted but glided over, then the mind is not troubled by any difficulty of reconciliation. There are even those who recommend this treatment as though Faith would be endangered by too close a consideration of the truth proposed to it. But the peace of mind thereby induced is a spurious peace. One strand of the mystery is allowed to fall into practical disuse, not bearing its proper fruit in the mental and spiritual life of the believer.

Karl Adam will have none of this. Christ was true God. Christ was true man. The mind will progress further and in the long run will find more solid peace if it squarely faces both truths, accepting both at their full value. The danger lies in wait for orthodox Catholics of concentrating on the Godhead of Christ and regarding the humanity as a sort of additional piece that does not quite fit in. Karl Adam must have the whole truth. There must be no seeping in of a practical monophysitism. Christ was true man, "like as we are in all things, yet without sin." Very well, let us study the man Christ *as* man. Inevitably this startles. But the measure in which it startles is the measure of the harm wrought in us by the compromise I have spoken of. We speak complacently of the Incarnation as a mystery— that is, as containing statements which we cannot reconcile —but as soon as we are brought face to face with these statements we recoil in alarm: our complacency is upset. How, we ask almost indignantly, can this picture of humanity be reconciled with the primary fact that Christ is God? How, indeed? But that precisely is why the doctrine of the Incarnation is called a mystery. Karl Adam has not created the problem. He has simply drawn attention to the other half of the doctrine. The shock that so many of us feel is comparable to the pain a man feels as the blood flows back into a frozen finger. A particular article of our belief had fallen out of use, and now it is brought back to life. We feel momentarily that our peace is upset. But we are wrong, numbness was not peace.

THE LOWER PANTHEISM

Chesterton as a poet has two master themes—he is a poet of motherhood and infancy, and he is a poet of battle. Since we are speaking of Chesterton, it would seem *de rigueur* to call this a paradox.

There is another fact also—which for the same strong reason and for no other under heaven—might be called by the same name: the two volumes of verse he has published with us are *The Queen of Seven Swords* and *Greybeards at Play*—the one a collection of poems on Our Lady, including "The Return of Eve," which, for any one who has meditated enough on the Fall of Man and the Immaculate Conception to read it at all, is one of the greatest religious poems in the language; the other—a superb piece of fooling of the sort that only Englishmen rejoice in, and that a Frenchman would die of shame to see attributed to himself.

Paradox the first I will not here discuss; it is difficult to talk at all to any one who finds it odd. But paradox the second is worth a closer look. The traditional assurance that it is only a step from the sublime to the ridiculous, is true, but needs completion by the further consideration that the step in question may be either perceived by the stepper or unperceived, with the result that he makes a fool either of some one else or of himself.

The difference between the sublime and the ridiculous lies not in the mind of the onlooker, but in the object perceived; and a fully-grown mind will move readily and with equal strength from one to another as its gaze shifts. The mind that is strongly and genuinely perceptive of (in addition to being merely sensitive to) the sublime, is so because it has a clear standard of the true order; and a mind with such a standard must be equally perceptive of disproportion and incongruity in things—that is, must have a sense of humour. (Wit is an analogous perception of incongruity in *words*; atheists are often wits, for they may well have a comprehended standard in words; but only theists are humorists, for only they have a comprehended standard in things.) The man who has a sense of the sublime, but none of the ridiculous, is only half a man; the man who sees the ridiculous, but not the sublime, is the other half.

Shakespeare had this completeness; so had Dickens. It was not in Milton, who was, in that sense, half a man (or perhaps three-quarters)—Thackeray being the other bit. It is terrifically strong in Chesterton—and he has brilliantly illustrated the theory in *The Napoleon of Notting Hill*.

Greybeards at Play, written forty years ago, and lately reprinted, is made up of three fables levelled against the three opponents who have so often felt the point of Chesterton's lance—the Pantheist, the Philanthropist and the Æsthete.

The method of the first may best be seen by comparison with certain lines of Wordsworth. For Wordsworth was of the type of "Pantheist who has never heard of Pan," and Chesterton applies the optimistic Wordsworth method to some of those parts of nature which Wordsworth quietly omitted as being difficult to square with his theory of Nature's "healing power."

Thus where Wordsworth cries:

> *To her fair works did Nature link*
> *The human soul that through me ran—*

Chesterton has:

> *I am akin to all the earth*
> *by many a tribal sign,*
> *The aged pig will often wear*
> *that sad sweet smile of mine.*

Where Wordsworth has:

> *And O ye fountains, meadows, hills and groves*
> *Think not of any severing of our loves*

Chesterton has:

> *And I have loved the Octopus*
> *since we were boys together;*
> *I love the Vulture and the Shark,*
> *I even love the weather.*

And as, at any rate, an echo of Wordsworth's

> *No motion has she now, no force;*
> *She neither hears, nor sees,*
> *Rolled round in earth's diurnal course*
> *With rocks and stones and trees*

compare the comprehensive

> *Come snow and hail, and thunderbolts,*
> *sleet, fire, and general fuss;*
> *Come to my arms, come all at once—*
> *oh photograph me thus!*

There is no space here to tell of *The Danger Attending Altruism on the High Seas* and *The Disastrous Spread of Æstheticism in All Classes.* But anyhow you know the sort of book it is, and it is most extravagantly illustrated by the author.

WHERE EXACTLY ARE WE?

I have always had my doubts about Scientists. I know that they are the humblest of all worshippers at the shrine of Truth, but I have never met one who had not a streak of the Circus Proprietor in him. In his own laboratory, where God forbid that I should ever see him, the Scientist may be the complete savant. But when he comes before the public, he undeniably loves to startle. He licks his lips to see our eyes grow rounder and rounder. He is a super-Barnum: only less vulgar. All nature is in his circus and the whole world is in his audience; but it is with a remote dry smile and not a loud bellow that he puts nature through its tricks for our amazement.

This element in the Scientist has grown enormously recently, but it has been there for a long time. I still remember the look on our science teacher's face as he told us that our bodies were 75% water (the fool of the class wondered that brainwaves were not more frequent). I have seen that look again and again as they have gone from atoms to protons and electrons, to neutrons, to positrons. We did not follow the details but we got the general notion: in the material universe, nothing is what it seems to us poor fish.

It is the special achievement of Freud to have done the same for the mind: in that sphere too what you find on the surface is utterly deceptive: the surface does no more than provide a handful of clues which guide the expert to the utterly different reality underneath: and indeed as a startler of the public the Psycho-analyst is as far beyond the Physicist as the Physicist was beyond Barnum. Your baby, for instance, seems like a baby to you: but it is a polymorphous sexual pervert: and you may think your own interest in gardening or stamp collecting or baseball or plainchant a sufficiently innocent matter but in fact it is only the masquerade in which lust finds its satisfying outlet.

As with physics, so with psycho-analysis: what the public made of it was not always precisely what the Master taught. But the public certainly made plenty of it. Everybody is talking Freud: only a couple of weeks ago I heard a girl on the bus complaining that her boy friend had an inferi-oddity complex: Heaven knows what significance Freud would have found in that mispronunciation. And higher on the educational ladder, the good public is more than half convinced that, repression being the one evil, sin is positively medicinal: one commits adultery now in the grave consciousness of a duty to one's health.

It is vital that Catholics should have clear minds about Freud. Mere dismissal is useless—he has become part of the atmosphere we must all breathe. That is why Rudolf Allers, himself an experimental psychologist, once prac-tising in Vienna and now teaching at the Catholic Univer-sity in Washington, has written *The Successful Error*. It is a condemnation of Freud's system but a condemnation based upon forty years of close study, the results of which he puts before us. Dr. Allers writes with authority after four to five hours a day for twenty years treating neurotic patients, teaching medical psychology, lecturing and writ-ing on psycho-analysis.

What is wrong with Freudism is in this book: also what is right with it. And even if you merely want to know what it is, you will find it here.

AN AFFAIR OF PERSPECTIVE

The poet who wrote of the illustrations to his own poems, that they

Make up in verve what they lack in perspective

expresses one of the difficulties that lie in wait for the worker in every art—verve is much easier to secure by not worrying too much about perspective. And as verve is what wins the multitude to a book, perspective is for too many writers no more than a poor relation. It is the merit of Ross Hoffman that he joins the two in equal wedlock. From first to last of *Restoration*, for example, he writes with a controlled passion which is one of the rarest of qualities: yet he gives a survey of world history over two thousand years which is a model of proportion.

His own line of approach to the church was historical. He became aware of the church first as a factor in history, then as *the* factor: passed slowly from dislike to liking, but still without suspecting any divine element in her. At last it did dawn upon him that natural explanations of the Church's existence and activity were so inadequate as to be absurd; and from that moment everything fell into place—world history had a pattern and a meaning, his own mind was suddenly at home and at ease. In this sense his conversion was a sheer fact, not to be analysed: it was something that happened to him. But though the experience as it actually befell him was unanalysable, he could not but turn to an analysis of the general relation of the Church to the world and to the human mind. He applies three tests—the test of origin to show that the Church of today is the Church Christ founded; the test of fruits, since a divine organism could not be in the world without producing effects proportionate to its nature; and the test of rationality, because man's mind is as much the work of God as the Church itself, and between any two of God's works there must be harmony.

Professor Hoffman's book must be classified with the work of Dawson, Berdyaev and Maritain. The man of today is being battered by facts—facts of history, psychology, and all the nine and ninety sciences. The mind is in danger of being battered to death with them. Nothing can save it but the possession of a total view to which each new fact can be referred—for judgment and ordination. Hoffman, like the leaders of the Catholic Revival, provides such a total view.

THE MODERN HILDEBRAND

W. S. Gilbert has a highly improbable link with the Papacy: The lines in *The Mikado*—

> *He always tries to utter lies*
> *And every time he fails—*

have been held to be a definition of Papal Infallibility and, as definitions go, one has heard worse. But there is a more striking reference. The man in *Pinafore* who stuck close to his desk and never went to sea and so became the ruler of the Queen's Navee was a pale anticipation of Pius XI, who at the time the lines were written was sticking very close to his desk indeed. To the age of sixty-one he was a librarian immersed in manuscripts—his main contact with the great world being in his subsidiary post as chaplain to a convent of nuns! Then Benedict XV sent him to the stormiest job the Church had on hand—the arrangement of some kind of ecclesiastical order in the new Poland, which in fact nearly plunged to its death while he was in Warsaw. Four years later he was Pope and after this unlikely apprenticeship found himself steering the Church through the mad world that very properly followed the mad war.

Such a career makes hay of all educational theories about preparing people for careers. One imagines the laughter if a British Prime Minister dragged out some modest convent chaplain to be his Foreign Secretary; and imagination fails at the thought of either of the great American parties presenting an elderly librarian as its candidate for the Presidency. Yet both Lord Halifax and Mr. Roosevelt would admit that their own job is easier than the Papacy in the world of today. But Achilles Ratti, carrying the burden of a rule begun before Mussolini or Hitler or Stalin or any of the men now in power in France or England or America and only ending last year, remained the one outstanding personality in a world that has never before known so many.

Popes are easy people to misunderstand. One reason applies even to Catholics. When Gregory the Great calls himself "servus servorum Dei", the servant of the servants of God, the non-Catholic thinks of the phrase as a piece of humility real or feigned. The Catholic knows that it is a literal fact. The Pope is there precisely for *our* convenience just like the dentist. Now we frequently dislike the ministrations of one as of the other, and wish that we might be served with less zeal. But here the parallel ends: for whereas we assume that the dentist knows his business better than we since we realise our ignorance of teeth, we assume that we know the Pope's business better than the Pope (for we none of us realise—indeed could scarcely realise without endangering the Constitution—our ignorance of world affairs). But there is a more profound reason for misunderstanding, and this applies to Pius XI more than to any of his predecessors for centuries. It was his contacts with the powers of this world that fill the newspapers: he entered into an unprecedented number of Concordats: he outfaced England over Malta, Mussolini over Catholic Youth Associations, Hitler over the new Paganism. It is easy to forget that all this front-page stuff was quite incidental, and that his real work in the purely spiritual sphere was not only more important in itself but occupied more of his mind. His action in declaring St. John of the Cross a Doctor of

the Church will still be governing men's minds twenty
centuries hence: when his rebuking of Hitler will be as forgotten as the Hitler he rebuked.

To both kinds of misunderstanding Father Hughes's
book, *Pope Pius XI*, is the answer. Here as nowhere else
we are made to face the vastness of the Pope's knowledge
of world affairs; and the immensity and the accuracy of the
information upon which he acted. His dealings with all the
great powers of the world are shown in their context. But
the greatest value of the book is in its careful examination
of every syllable of what may be called his purely religious
pronouncements—on seminaries, on studies, on spirituality.
The reader is given the chance to understand the Pope:
not to understand him means not to see anything in world
affairs quite as it is.

THE SWEET SINGER OF ISRAEL

It was Samuel Butler—the one from whom Bernard Shaw got most of his ideas—who said that if the Psalms had been published for the first time in his own day the bookstores would not have taken more than a dozen copies unless they took a chance on its royal authorship getting it something of a sale. If that be simply one of Butler's gibes, Catholics at least cannot fling it back in his teeth. For we are not great readers of the Psalms.

There is something more curious still. Priests read the whole hundred-and-fifty psalms through every week of their lives. Most of them probably spend more time reading the Psalms than on all other reading put together. Now the Psalms have a very strong, very definite atmosphere of their own: come upon even a verse of a Psalm in the midst of a page of something else, and it seems like the only sentence on the page. You would expect that men thus apparently immersed in that strong atmosphere, as priests are, would have their speech and their writing unmistakably marked by it—I don't mean be-spangled with quotations from the Psalms but somehow influenced in their movement and cadence and structure by them. Yet they do not: they have kept their speech and their writing unspotted from the Psalms.

Both facts are odd because of the range and mightiness of the Psalms. It is a mere commonplace that they leave no human emotion unexpressed. There is nothing the human soul can be thirsting to say that they do not say. What, then, comes between us and them? It is this barrier that Father

Martindale's book *Towards Loving the Psalms* seeks to discover and to remove.

It would be idle to try to summarize a book that may very well outlive all the rest of Father Martindale's works. But we can at least indicate where he finds the barrier. It lies in this—that our twentieth century is the most provincial age of the world's history, an age more incapable than any other of entering into a spirit not its own. This insularity—perhaps it is the same that has exiled Greek and Latin from our schools—is an evil in that it shuts away from us the very food our souls most need, solely because it is in a container of a pattern unfamiliar to us. It is Father Martindale's aim, therefore, first to get his imagination and then to get ours *somewhat in the state of the author's own.* How brilliantly he does it we can barely indicate.

Take the less important matter of external nature: "The Hebrew mind didn't appreciate, one would say, *small* things. Job has any amount about the crocodile and the hippopotamus but nothing about butterflies . . . There is much about light but little about colors. . . ."

All this is fascinating but it is when we come to the human psychology of the Hebrew that the book is at its grandest. Thus:

"We, mild in our reactions, must remember the immediate and furious reaction of the oriental. In bad moments, his soul sticks to the dust; his bones are like clods scattered over the earth; he vanishes like a shadow as it dwindles, he can be shaken off as you shake a locust from your dress; he is flattened down into the dust and his heart is glued to the earth."

There remains the problem of the so-called cursing psalms—very remote, so we feel, from the spirit of Christ.

Some of this Father Martindale sees as simply a species of "war dialect"—the ancient Hebrew liked to describe himself as hewing his way up to his knees in blood. But in so far as these expressions are more than a fashion of speech, here is Father Martindale's explanation:

"We can say that at least to some extent men *must* be the children of their period. We repeat that the Hebrews were not in the least a perfect race; they were being led forward in the line of goodness by great men who saw further (under God's illumination) than they did, but (perhaps fortunately) not too much further. It seems to be God's plan to pick up men where they are, and lead them somewhat further, but not all the way."

Such was Christ's own method. The goal lay further than His disciples guessed; *their* great work was to carry men further towards it than at first they knew.

"It matters less from what emotions the Hebrew started than what ideas or emotions were in conflict with, and continuously modifying, his erroneous self. Towards what was the Hebrew mentality growing? Into what did it, at its best, emerge? Into something so sweet and pure that no pagan race has ever had anything to put into serious competition with it."

THE SPLENDOR OF THE LITURGY

Wordsworth's

> *The moon doth with delight*
> *Look round her when the heavens are bare*

and Virgil's "Sunt lachrymae rerum" witness over eighteen hundred years to the same truth: the poets cannot be happy with the idea that nature is dead. They feel the life in it, though they do not always know what the life is that they feel. The Christian is exactly the reverse: he knows what the mystery is, but for the most part does not feel it. He knows as a fact of Christian doctrine that God is at the very centre of all things whatsoever, sustaining them by His own continuing life above the surface of that nothingness from which He drew them.

If you see anything whatever—the merest speck of dust even—without seeing the infinite energy that lives in it to sustain it in being, you are seeing it wrong. This we know as a matter of doctrine but we do not *experience* things in that way; we are like Wordsworth's Peter Bell:

> *A primrose by a river's brim*
> *A yellow primrose was to him*
> *And it was nothing more.*

We see the surface of things, are content with the surface, grow bored with the surface.

That is why there has to be a liturgical movement. The liturgy sees all natural things as expressing the enormous energy of God: *we* see them as so much dead matter—nothing so gay, even, as a primrose—bread, wine, water, stone, chasubles, incense. The consecrated species are a living reality; but the rest is the ceremonial handling of lifeless things.

It is the aim of Father Zundel's *The Splendor of the Liturgy* to make the liturgy come alive to us by making creation come alive to us, by making us see every created thing "outlined against this mysterious background of invisible light, in which the interior of its being is revealed —what it owes to the thought and receives from the love of God." This is the plain truth of things. And with this truth as guide he takes us through the liturgy of the Mass —every object used, every action, every word spoken, the golden silences. In the Mass we are handling immensities and it is the marvel of the unbeliever that we handle them almost casually—God is being offered on the altar and we are making spasmodic efforts against distraction. No one will read Father Zundel's book and stay casual; even if not all will reach that high point he desiderates where the soul becomes aware in the liturgy of "the most intimate tones and the most secret heart-beats of God's own life."

THE HUMAN SIDE

We Catholics have built up an unanswerable apologetic that proves the Church to be a divine institution. But it does not explain the Church as a human institution. Non-Catholics cannot answer our arguments, but equally they cannot stomach *us*: they could swallow Catholicism if they could swallow Catholics. They feel that the fact of us excuses them from the necessity of answering our arguments.

It is the real point of Edward Watkin's book, *The Catholic Centre,* that it does take account of the Church *as she actually is here and now*: not simply an ideal in the mind of Christ, but an ideal working in and through the defective human beings who, at any moment, constitute the hierarchy and laity of her visible body on earth. This is what the world sees; and the difficulty the world finds in reconciling what it thinks the Church ought to be, with what it sees under its eyes, is the supreme apologetic problem. There is no other problem so acute; and we know of no other book that treats it.

Our apologists do, of course, mention the human side of the Church: but too often this means simply a discussion of "bad Catholics." Now bad Catholics, even bad popes, are scarcely a problem at all. It is good Catholics that make the problem. The question that the individual puts to himself—"Why am I not more worthy of the truths I know?"—strikes the outsider in the tragically different form "How can these things be true if Catholics are like that?"

This most superficial part of the problem Watkin of course treats. But he plunges much deeper. It is not only the Catholic *will* that falls short of the known standard. The Catholic *intellect* too finds it hard to keep the perfect balance and at any given moment may show a slackened appreciation of some aspect of revealed truth, some variation from the perfect centrality of Catholic doctrine.

But to do this effectively he must show that Catholic doctrine possesses this centrality. This he does massively, by making a survey of the warring ideas that rend the world—materialism and idealism, individualism and communism, and a dozen other pairs—and showing how, in regard to each such pair, the Catholic doctrine contains what is true in each and rejects what is false. But if Catholic doctrine *in itself* thus holds the perfect balance, Catholic doctrine as it exists in the mind and energies and in the actions of Catholics at any given moment is liable to swing away a little from the centre. I take a minor example from his book because it can be stated shortly: in the teaching of the Church, and most wonderfully in her liturgy, the Crucifixion is balanced by the Resurrection and the Ascension. But on the walls of our Churches the Crucifixion is everything, Resurrection and Ascension appearing, if at all, only somewhere among the stained glass.

In one phase, this book is as searching an examination of the Catholic conscience as has ever been made by a Catholic. Upon us who are of the household of the faith the effect is astonishingly stimulating; upon non-Catholics we believe it will have an effect just as astonishing for, whereas many books have answered the objections they have raised, this book will answer objections which they have never actually formulated, but which hang in their minds as a sort of unanalyzed cloud through which the sun simply cannot break.

FIRST THINGS

Having heard for years past the slogan "Truth in Advertising," and feeling that my mind could do with a little truth, I turned to the advertising columns of the weekly in my hand at the critical moment and found this:

Men who put first things first in their thinking naturally look upon Bass's Ale as an important discovery.

So no doubt it is: so no doubt also are Ruppert's Beer, Kellogg's Corn Flakes and Wrigley's Chewing Gum—*most* important discoveries, all of them. Only it is not obvious what any of them *or* Bass have to do with putting first things first in one's thinking. And as a close listener to other men's words, I find that this is almost always what happens: there is a grand flourish of trumpets about putting first things first: most of those who urge us thus grandiloquently would not know a first thing if they saw one; and the grand flourish ends in a plea for something so far down the list—a hair-restorer or a politician or an economic system—that no number has been assigned to it.

Yet the mere repetition of the phrase indicates a kind of thirst that even Bass cannot slake: a thirst for order in thinking as an indispensable preliminary to order in action. That thirst exists in the human spirit, but most of us do not know what it is that thus troubles us: we know it merely as a thirst—we do not know what it is a thirst for —and indeed are as likely as not to try to quench it with Bass—which is very good for the manufacturer, and very agreeable for the drinker, but leaves this special thirst much where it was. Yet daily experience in so odd

a world should give us the clue; a man who found himself
in a cart that had been placed before the horse should
guess, even if he had never seen either a cart or a horse
before, that the order was somehow wrong.

Order in action is vital; order in action is impossible
without order in thinking; one of the great masters of
order in thinking is St. Thomas Aquinas. That is why we
are delighted that the Dominican Fathers of St. Joseph's
Province are producing a new quarterly *The Thomist*. It
will examine the deepest-lying principles of human action
to find what they imply and how they may be further applied; it will examine concrete problems, sort out the principles involved in them, examine these principles, recom-
bine them. It is not solely for philosophers and theologians.
It will deal with problems that concern all men. Its object
will be to bring the educated layman too within the circle
of light cast by St. Thomas.

To conclude as we began—almost—Men who look upon
The Thomist as an important discovery will come naturally to put first things first in their thinking—unless they
are congenitally incapable of so great a variation from the
average.

THE GREATNESS OF ST. BENEDICT

If Europe is worth having, then the world owes a measureless debt to the monasteries. As the Roman Empire sank to its decline, the Church in Europe found herself in a world of utter chaos; with barbarism and the rending of the social order all about her, in a Europe that had less social or even racial unity than Asia has now, the Church had to swim by her own strength or else sink and with her the civilization of the Europe that was to be. What the Papacy meant in such a chaos there is no space to tell here; but the Papacy would have been powerless to save civilization without the monks—above all the monks who came pouring into Europe from Ireland first and then from England. Outside the monasteries intellectual life scarcely existed; and indeed—if intellectual life itself be held a luxury in such an age—even the arts and crafts had no other home. Towns still existed, but sadly reduced and of no great functional importance; society was almost entirely agrarian.

It is easy to see what the monasteries meant in such a time. Facing the agrarian problem with a fullness of energy that could have come only from men who held their lands as God's lands, they cleared forests and drained marshes which otherwise must only have remained waste: certainly the "profit-motive" could never have brought individual settlers to success in tasks so heartbreaking as the great monastic communities normally shouldered. Further, as Christopher Dawson writes (in *The Making of Europe*): "The monasteries were not only great agricultural centres, they were also centres of trade; and thanks to the immunities which they enjoyed they were able to establish markets, to coin money and even to develop a system of credit. They fulfilled in a primitive fashion the function of banks and insurance societies."

All this being matter of common knowledge, how great a role in the history of civilization is St. Benedict's? He was not the founder of monasticism; the great Irish monks who began the work of the re-making of Europe before the Benedictines lived by other rules; but as the years went by the rule he gave superseded others and by the beginning of the eighth century European monasticism was Benedictine. In a day when European civilization (with its worldwide provinces) is, if not in dissolution, at any rate filled with self-distrust, unsure of its own principles, and submitting its roots to question, we should look again at St. Benedict who watered those roots when there was little prospect of flower or fruit. Dom Justin McCann, a monk of Ampleforth, has given us in *St. Benedict* the most admirable modern picture. Certainly the Saint was not thinking in any terms so grandiose as the re-making of Europe; that great matter was simply a by-product of something else—the desire of a lover of God to provide a way of life for other lovers of God.

PHILIP OF SPAIN

It is the very mark of the provincial mind that it thinks its own village is the whole world. The provincial of today knows, so widely has education spread, that there actually are other places. But he has no mental measure for them. He can imagine nothing beyond the level of Muddleton: to that level everything is scaled down. Talk to your provincial of Shakespeare and the glory of great poetry, and he mentions that his daughter writes a bit of verse (some of it got printed in the local paper); talk to him of Mozart and the glory of great music, and he tells you that the minister's wife played the piano at the last Church social; talk to him of Helen of Troy and he is reminded that the girl at the drugstore is a bit flighty. Just as he measures the grandeur of things by what he has experienced in Muddleton, so he measures their possibility: what has not happened there, cannot happen. And Muddleton is not necessarily a village: it is a state of mind. Talk to your provincial of a Virgin Birth and he disposes of the matter very simply: there's never been one in Muddleton. Tell him, if he be at once a scientist and a provincial, of bread and wine changed at a word into body and blood: he disposes of that as simply—it's never been done in his laboratory. Village, small town, metropolis—yokel, captain of industry, scientist—provincialism is everywhere and in all men the same defect: they live happily complacent within the horizon of their own experience, and by its meagreness they measure all reality.

There is no more cruel test for the twentieth century provincial than to be faced with Philip II of Spain. He is a fascinating study in an extinct psychology, the psychology of hereditary absolute monarchy. From within the horizon of nineteenth century liberalism, you cannot hope to understand him. Nor is he of the same sort as the modern dictators, whom he would have regarded as sheer monstrosities! The Englishman who dismisses Philip II as a Hitler who happened to have religion—the American who, looking upon some of Philip's problems, asks what would Calvin Coolidge have done?—are typical Muddleton citizens. What they have to say is useful to a student of their psychology but throws no light on Philip's. They are all Yankees at the court of King Arthur.

William Thomas Walsh who has written a most brilliant life of Philip has escaped the provincial pitfall—he gets miraculously close to seeing things as Philip saw them. Thus upon the question whether Philip killed his son Don Carlos, or his third wife Queen Isabel, or his brother Don John of Austria, Walsh sees what few historians have seen—that Philip would never have questioned his legal and moral right as king to kill any one of them. If he had killed all three his conscience, though it was an unusually tender conscience, would not have missed a beat.

As the book settles in the mind, we realise that we have lived through a whole world—a world out of which our own has grown. Everything in the twentieth century—from Mickey Mouse to Stalin—is understood better if we grasp what was happening in the sixteenth. And we are a long stride away from our native provincialism for the experience. To have met Philip in this intimate way is an education. The Church is more Catholic for having had Philip II; and we are more Catholic for realising him as our coreligionist.

RESOLUTION TO SUICIDE

Few men have lived a double life as thoroughly as Dr. Halliday Sutherland. The public first knew him as the antagonist of Dr. Marie Stopes, who is the apostle of Birth Control. Her unsuccessful libel action against him in the House of Lords remains the outstanding English legal event in Contraception's chequered history since the famous case of Bradlaugh and Annie Besant. Then, out of a blue sky, came his *Arches of the Years*, a book of reminiscences which made its rapid way to the best-seller front by sheer charm. The public rubbed its eyes and thought it must be a different Sutherland coincidentally named Halliday. It was obviously indicated that sooner or later a book should combine both Sutherlands. *Laws of Life* is it. It is written easily and lightened with personal reminiscence. It treats of some of the gravest biological laws that concern individuals and races. In a way, it bears the same relation to biology that Sir James Jeans's *Mysterious Universe* bears to astronomy.

He begins with the mystery of conception, the relation between the sexes in which it is enfolded, the growth and development of the individual human being—"who biologically has no parents but four grandparents." The relation to all this of contraception and periodic abstinence is discussed as an affair not of ethics but of science. Arising from this discussion is the question of heredity. Here again certain scientific laws appear, significant in themselves, still more significant in their suggestion of greater laws behind them as yet unknown to us. As a pendant to this section, the Sterilization of the Unfit is examined from a great many angles. On all these matters one is constantly reminded of Chesterton's praise: "If we could be as indecent in our language as they are immoral in their conclusions, we could smash them." Dr. Sutherland maintains the decencies of language; yet one feels that some smashing is being done.

The later part of the book concerns itself with those mysterious laws which govern the growth and decline of population. The Law of Malthus is shown for what it is— a fallacy which it is sheerly fantastic that anyone should ever have taken seriously. But again there are laws—curious, unlikely laws. There are laws found by experiment upon the animal kingdom—some of these experiments are described—which history suggests are fully applicable to men. Communities will die: but they will die all the quicker for those governmental activities which seek to use death as a means to save them. Contraception, sterilisation, euthanasia and such like are a direct assault upon life, and life will not be saved by them. Dr. Sutherland already finds the danger signals in Western Europe and the United States; but at the end of all the study of biological laws, one faces the free human will. If only one could feel certain that it will stir. For, as he says "The suicide of a race demands less resolution than the suicide of an individual."

STRAY REMARKS

I

Belloc has been all his life a maker of roads. Also he irritates many people. The two things go together. The maker of roads must use a pneumatic-drill, and this is a nerve-shattering instrument. If the preservation of your nerves is your first consideration, you will wish he would stop. If you grasp the importance of the roads to be made, you will wish more power to his elbow. In nothing has his very powerful genius been more evident than in the diagnosis of what he has called *The Servile State*. Thirty years ago he saw the way we were going. And the thirty years since have seen his worst prophecies gloomily fulfilled. He thinks that we may still be saved by a wider distribution of property: in *The Restoration of Property* he considers how this may be brought about; and in nothing does he show himself more of a realist than in his discussion of whether men in general have not gone too far along the road of slavery (which offers itself as Security) even to desire property—which carries with it the dangerous word Responsibility.

II

When Milton wrote:

Avenge, O Lord, Thy slaughtered Saints,

he was not calling down a curse on the writers of saints' lives. Yet many a saint has suffered more from his biographer than from his persecutors. The fathers stone the prophets, and the sons build the monuments: and often the monuments ought to be stoned too. This, if done as an act of reparation to the dead, is a pious act, but it should not be done merely to relieve the feelings. The best thing of all is to ignore the unworthy monument and build a worthy. To adapt a phrase of Pugin's—to write the life of a saint badly, a man must try very hard. What is the secret of bad hagiography? The falsetto voice, I fancy—which is not necessarily an excited treble; a deep bass can be as falsetto as any treble. Anyhow, our own age can show a number of good, and a handful of great, saints' lives.

THE LIFE OF OUR LORD

The life of Our Lord can be got only from the Gospels. The trouble is that most of us cannot get it from the Gospels because, in a day when everybody can read, almost nobody can read very well. We can get what is written on the page; but what is not written we don't get.

I'm sorry if this sounds obscure. Look at it like this. If a certain statement is true, then certain other things which it implies must also be true. Thus if you are told that a man went out in the rain without coat or umbrella, you do not need to be told that he got wet: if anyone adds that he got wet, then he is assuming that you are a person of mean intelligence. You have to be told.

Our newspapers are run on this principle: (HEADLESS BODY FOUND: POLICE SUSPECT FOUL PLAY). So are our novels. Galsworthy describes a funeral: "The hearse moved off slowly. The carriages followed at a foot's pace." In other words it was a funeral. Not a chariot race. Perhaps we feel that such instances really are an insult to our intelligence. But once we get beyond the most obvious implications, most of us have to be told. Now the Gospels were written by Matthew and the others for people who could read. Anything that was necessarily implied in what they wrote did not get written. It did not have to.

But it does now. And this has been the tragedy of many of the writers of lives of Our Lord. They were no better at reading than the majority of people. They could read what was written: but they were not good at reading what was unwritten. Therefore, to justify their writing a Life at all, they filled in by imagining what it seemed to them should have happened—what Our Lord felt like, what went on in His soul. But imagining what God-made-man felt like is a dangerous business; it boils down in practice to imagining what the author would have felt like had he been God-made-man. No one can do that.

Who would ever have imagined the Agony in the Garden, if it had not been written in the Gospels? When we read what Christ actually did do, we recognize (sometimes a little obscurely) its perfect rightness; but we would never have thought of it for ourselves. Therefore the imaginative writers fail; if they express the devotional atmosphere of the moment, they hold their readers for the moment. But who ever reads a life of Our Lord written twenty years ago?

The excellence of Father Vincent McNabb is that because he has the vision to see so much of what is there, he has no need to invent or embroider. In his *Life of Our Lord* he looks at the Gospels and tells us what he sees. To take the tiniest instance, he notes that the whip with which Our Lord cleansed the temple of its money-changers is the only thing he is recorded as having *made*. There is nothing in his book that is not in the Gospels. It's not all written there. But it's all there. And we would not have found it. Twenty years will not see this book staled.

FEMINISM

At the beginning of her life of St. Catherine of Siena, Alice Curtayne has an instructive sentence: how in the Middle Ages "Women occasionally soared into a freedom which makes modern feminism look foolish. They did not do it by suffrage or by adopting boyish dress, but by cutting the thongs of their own futility." For a commentary on this sentence, read *St. Joan* by Stanislas Fumet, and *St. Margaret Mary* by Henri Ghéon. For here are two emancipated women—the less emancipated of the two being the one who meddled in politics.

It may seem odd to link two women so superficially unlike; but in Catholicism is perpetually realized Bacon's definition of the poetic gift—the perception of similitude in dissimilitude. The Colonel's lady and Judy O'Grady are sisters under their skin: because (whether Kipling knew it or not) they were both children of one Father; and obviously the closer people are to their common Father, the closer they are to each other; which makes the saints closest of all, practically blood relations, but these two saints especially.

To insist on surface differences would be a waste of time. Joan led an army and crowned a king; Margaret Mary was a nun in an enclosed order. Even the flame which came to both alike is there for contrast and not likeness; for Joan died in her flame and Margaret Mary lived in hers.

Yet they were engaged in the same task. Why did God work the unique miracle He worked through Joan, a thing quite without parallel in all His dealings with men? Why all this whirr of supernatural activity to put the

miserable Charles on the throne of France? "The mountains are in labor, and they bring forth a ridiculous mouse"
—so sang Horace, and he never contemplated a mouse
more ridiculous than Charles. Joan knew the answer, if
Charles did not. The throne of France might be pitiful if
held by a pitiful king; but even held by the greatest of
kings, it was still earthly and would pass. We are back at
Claudel's principle again.* Joan was not concerned to make
Charles king: but to make the King of France God's
viceroy. Every T of her mission was crossed and every I
dotted by Margaret Mary: as Henri Ghéon shows.

.These two small books are naturally not solely concerned
with such high matters. After all, the authors did not
write them in consultation. What each produces is an extraordinarily poignant story—not chaptered or dovetailed
but each flung out in one jet—told as it were in one breath.
Of Henri Ghéon who concentrates in this prose-poem all
that he has had to say on sanctity anywhere, there is no
need to speak. Stanislas Fumet, author of *Joan*, is a French
publisher: how many publishers write like that?

* See above, pages 91-2.

BAD NEWS FOR CAMELS

Nothing is so mysterious psychologically as the attitude of the Catholic in the world to Our Lord's warnings about riches. He has warned us with appalling clarity of the risk of damnation that goes with being rich. Yet those among us who are poor strive for riches, cheerfully willing to take the risk; while the rich thank Him for the warning, drop an extra dollar in the plate, and thereafter can look a needle in the eye with never a blush. One immediate effect of Dorothy Day's *House of Hospitality* is that it makes the needle's eye look horribly small—much smaller than the camel thought—as small as it is. For here is the reality of poverty.

In face of poverty we all have a duty. Dorothy Day interpreted her duty pretty strictly: she must go among the poor, but not as a visitor, however devoted, from outside. She must go among the poor as Father Damien went among the lepers—to stay. She must become poor, as he became a leper—not with the decent, orderly, dignified poverty of self-denial, but with the real poverty of the poor. At her House of Hospitality in Mott Street hundreds sleep roughly and eat meagrely, and so does she.

Any journalist can go into the slums and return with a dozen picturesque or heart-rending stories. Jack London did it for the London slums in *People of the Abyss;* it has been done for share-croppers, Kentucky miners, Pittsburgh steel-workers. But always by people who are, with all respect to them, trippers. They come; they see; they depart. Dorothy Day is unique. She is not only the writer observing the poor with the fine-strung sensibility of the artist;

with that same sensibility, she is one of the poor who are being observed. To use a comparison from another field: Hemingway writes magnificently of a bull fight: but suppose Hemingway could become the bull, while retaining his Hemingway power to feel and express. What sort of an epic would you expect?

I feel that I am failing to state her special quality. I shall take one more shot at expressing it. In this book poverty utters itself, the poor become articulate, through the mouth of Dorothy Day. There are a dozen stories as horrible or heroic as you would find on Molokai. But through them all you feel, as an almost physical oppression, the terrible patience of the poor. And it is her greatest gift that she has herself acquired it.

BIOGRAPHICAL NOTES

ADAM, KARL. Born 1876 at Pursruck in Bavaria. Educated Classical Gymnasium, Amberg and Theological College at Ratisbon. Ordained 1900. Two years' parish work. Studied Patrology and History of Dogma at Munich University; 1915, Professor Extraordinary at same university; 1917, Professor of Moral Theology, Strasbourg; 1919, Professor of Dogmatic Theology at Tübingen. Besides patristic studies, his principal works are: *The Spirit of Catholicism, Christ our Brother* and *Jesus Christus* (which appears in English as *The Son of God*). *The Spirit of Catholicism* has had an immense effect on thought both inside and outside the Church.

ALLERS, RUDOLF, M.D. Reader in Psychiatry at the University of Vienna. Now Professor at Catholic University, Washington, D. C. As an experimental psychologist follows Alfred Adler, but with his own modifications. Has effected a real synthesis of scholastic and modern experimental psychology. Works of his translated into English are *The Psychology of Character* (also published in a shortened and simplified form as *Practical Psychology*) and *The New Psychologies*. He wrote *The Successful Error* in English.

ARENDZEN, REV. JOHN, D.D., Ph.D., M.A. Born in Amsterdam 1873, and educated at Oscott. He graduated in Theology at Munich and Philosophy at Bonn: research degree at Christ's College, Cambridge, England. He is a member of the Catholic Mission Society and Spiritual Director at St. Edmund's College, Ware, since 1937; published the Syriac text of the Apostolic Church Order 1901. He is the author of *Gospels: Fact, Myth, or Legend? Prophets, Priests, and Publicans; What Becomes of the Dead? Men and Manners in the Days of Christ; Whom do You Say; Reason and Religion; The Holy Trinity* and articles in Cambridge and Continental learned journals and in Catholic Encyclopaedia.

BELLOC, HILAIRE. Born 1870 at St. Cloud, France. Educated in England at the Oratory School and Oxford. In between he did his conscript service in the French army. From Oxford he came to London as a journalist, began to write books, married an American, Elodie Hogan, naturalized English 1902, sat in House of Commons 1905-10. He wrote *The Bad Child's Book of Beasts* in 1896 and is a master of this kind of children's verse. He has written in almost every literary genre, and we can do no more here than suggest some of his most characteristic work. (1) Biography: *Danton, Robespierre, Marie Antoinette, Richelieu, Cranmer;* (2) Belles Lettres: *Avril, Path to Rome, Caliban's Guide to Letters, The Cruise of the Nona;* (3) Essays: *The Four Men, The Silence of the Sea;* (4) Sociology: *Servile State, Restoration of Property;* (5) Political Novels: *Emmanuel Burden, Mr. Clutterbuck's Election;* (6) A group of novels illustrated by Chesterton, of which the best known is *Mr. Petre;* (7) *The History of England,* of which Vols. I to IV are now published; *Characters of the Reformation;* (8) Apologetic; *Companion to Wells' Outline of History, Essays of a Catholic;* (9) Military Science: *Strategy and Tactics of Marlborough Campaign of 1812;* (10) Poetry: *Sonnets and Verse.*

BERDYAEV, NICOLAS ALEXANDROVICH. Born in Kiev, 1874; exiled to North of Russia in 1899 and threatened with banishment 1917 for criticizing subservience of Russian Orthodox Church to civil power. Bolsheviks appointed him Professor of Philosophy in University of Moscow but in 1922 after two terms of imprisonment, they expelled him as an upholder of religion. He lives in Paris, directs the Academy of the Philosophy of Religion (which he founded) and edits a review entitled *Putj* (The Way). His first book, *Subjectivism and Individualism in Social Philosophy,* appeared in 1900. In 1916 appeared *The Meaning of the Creative Work.* Translated into English are *The End of Our Time, Dostoievsky, Christianity and Class War.*

BLONDEL, MAURICE. Born 1861, at Dijon. Professor of Philosophy at Aix-en-Provence. His book *L'Action*, caused a very great stir among Catholics in the mid-nineties of the last century, as did his *Lettre sur les exigences de la Pensée contemporaine en matière d'apologétique*. Certain of his ideas have had a powerful influence on the development of present-day scholasticism.

BLOY, LEON. Born 1846 at Perigeux. After agnostic and unhappy youth went to Paris to paint. Became the secretary of Barbey d'Aurevilly, through whom he took up literature. Later converted. Lived in utmost poverty after the war of 1870. Was a railway official from 1877 to 1888, when he wrote *Le Désepéré*. Translated into English are *Letters to His Fiancée* and the novel *The Woman Who Was Poor*. Died in 1916.

CHARLOT, JEAN. See page 59.

CHESTERTON, G. K. Born in 1874, educated St. Paul's School, London. Studied art at the Slade School, illustrated his own first book, *Greybeards at Play*, and continued to illustrate books for his friend Belloc. As a journalist, early became associated in the public mind with his brother Cecil and with Belloc in two fields—in sociology as an enemy of the Servile State, and in religion as a champion of Catholicism, though he did not enter the Church till 1922. Like Belloc, wrote in most genres. His fantastic novels (such as the *Napoleon of Notting Hill*) and the detective stories concerned with Fr. Brown have had immense success. For a rapid access to his thought one might read *Orthodoxy*, *St. Francis of Assisi*, *The Everlasting Man*, *St. Thomas Aquinas* and his *Autobiography*. Sociologically he was the inspiration of the Distributist Movement. He died in 1936.

CLAUDEL, PAUL. Born 1868 at Villeneuve-sur-Fère, in Northern France. Finished his school career at eighteen, completely under influence of Taine, Renan and scientific materialism. In 1886 was first awakened to the supernatural by the reading of Rimbaud's

Illuminations, by 1890 he was in the Church. In the French Diplomatic Service, stationed in Germany, China, Denmark, Japan, Brazil, Japan again, Ambassador at Washington till 1933. Now Ambassador at Brussels. His work roughly divisible into (a) Lyric Poetry—note especially *Cinq Grandes Odes, Cantate à Trois Voix, Corona benignitatis anni Dei;* (b) Drama—note the very difficult *Tête d'Or, L'Otage, L'Annonce faite à Marie, Le Soulier de Satin.* These last two have been published in English, as has also a collection of essays under the title *Ways and Crossways.*

CURTÁYNE, ALICE. Her first book, *St. Catherine of Siena,* made her instantly famous. Educated at the Convent of La Sainte Union, Southampton. Lived some time in Italy, came to England and was one of the outdoor speakers of the Catholic Evidence Guild. Returned to her home in Trales, Co. Kerry, in 1928. Has lived there since. Her principal works are *A Recall to Dante, St. Anthony of Padua, St. Brigid of Ireland.*

DAWSON, CHRISTOPHER. Born 1889. Educated Winchester and Oxford. Entered the Church 1914. Already at Oxford he had begun to make a special study of the relations of religion, sociology and culture, and in this field lies his life work. His thesis is best set out in *Progress and Religion.* The best known of his historical works are *The Age of The Gods* and *The Making of Europe;* of his sociological works, *Religion and the Modern State* and *Beyond Politics.* Has published a collection of essays under the title *Enquiries into Religion and Culture* and has written two small books (*Christianity and the New Age* and *The Modern Dilemma*) for the series of *Essays in Order* of which he is joint editor.

DAY, DOROTHY. Born 1898 Brooklyn. Educated Univ. of Illinois. Worked for Communist Party. Joined the Church 1927. With Peter Maurin founded the first House of Hospitality, in 1932 in New York. Similar houses have since been founded all over the country.

Edits the *Catholic Worker.* Has written *From Union Square to Rome* and *House of Hospitality.*

FARRELL, REV. WALTER, O.P. Born in Chicago, Illinois, 1902. Ordained 1927. Took degree of Doctor of Theology at Fribourg, Switzerland, 1930. Since then has been Professor of Theology at Dominican House of Studies, Washington, D. C. Appointed Regent of Studies for the Province of St. Joseph in 1939. In 1940, after special examination in Rome, received highest theological degree in Dominican Order, Master of Sacred Theology.

FARREN, ROBERT. Irish Poet, known perhaps better as Roibeard O. Fearachain. Born Dublin some thirty years ago. Taught in Dublin schools till recent appointment as Director of Irish Language broadcasts on Radio Eireann.

FEENEY, REV. LEONARD, S.J. Born in Lynn, Massachusetts, 1897. Entered Society of Jesus in 1914. Educated Woodstock College, Oxford. Ordained 1928. Now Literary Editor of *America.* Books: *In Towns and Little Towns, Riddle and, Reverie, Boundaries, Song for a Listener,* all poetry; and *Fish on Friday, You'd Better Come Quietly,* prose.

GHEON, HENRI. Born 1875. Educated at Lycée at Sens and as medical student in Paris. Lost his Faith in his early teens. From 1901-1909 country doctor in his birthplace, Bray-sur-Seine. Helped found *Nouvelle Revue Française.* Served in the French army for the four years of the War. Returned to the Faith 1915. Decided to write plays on the lives of the Saints. Since 1920 has written forty (*The Comedian, The Marvellous History of St. Bernard, The Marriage of St. Francis* have appeared in English). In 1925, founded the Compagnons de Notre Dame to act them. Acts in them himself. Wrote a three-volume novel, *Les Jeux de l'Enfer et du Ciel.* His studies of the Curé d'Ars, St. Thérèse of Lisieux, St. John Bosco, St. Margaret Mary, and St. Vincent Ferrer have also appeared in English.

GILSON, Etienne. Born in France 1884; graduated at Sorbonne with degree of Docteur-ès-lettres; taught at Universities of Lille, Strasbourg and Paris. Professor at Collège de France since 1935; began lecturing at Institute of Mediaeval Studies, Toronto, in 1929; gave Gifford Lectures at Aberdeen, James Lectures at Harvard; editor of collection of Etudes de Philosophie Mediévale. Books translated into (or written in) English are: *Principles of Mediaeval Philosophy*, *Philosophy of St. Bonaventure*, *Mystical Theology of St. Bernard*, *Christianity and Philosophy*.

DE GRANDMAISON, Léonce, S.J. Born 1858. Novitiate S.J., Slough (England). Ordained 1898. Took important part in Modernist controversies, and was one of the creators of the science of Comparative Religion as Catholics see it. 1913 contributed 30,000 word article, *Jésus Christ*, to Dictionnaire d'Apologétique. This was the ground plan of his monumental work of the same name. Died 1927.

HOFFMAN, Ross, J. S. Born in Harrisburg, Pennsylvania, 1903. Studied at Lafayette, Columbia and Pennsylvania State College. Now Professor of History at New York University. Awarded the George Louis Beer prize of the American Historical Association for his monograph on European International Relations, Great Britain and the German Trade Rivalry 1875-1914. Came into the Church about 1932. Author of *Restoration, The Will to Freedom* and *The Organic State*.

HUGHES, Rev. Philip. Born in Manchester in 1895, was educated at St. Bede's, Manchester, Ushaw, Leeds, and Louvain University (Lic. en sciences hist. 1921) and ordained a priest in 1920. He undertook historical research work in Rome from 1921 to 1923. He was a lecturer in History at the College of St. Thomas, St. Paul, Minnesota from 1923 to 1924. Was a parish priest in Manchester, England from 1924 to 1931, and has since been archivist of Westminster. He is the author of *The Catholic Question, 1688 to 1829, History of the Church* (Vol. I: *The Church and the World in*

Which It Was Founded; Vol. II: *The Church and the World It Created*), *Pius XI*.

JOYCE, GEORGE HAYWARD, S.J. Born 1864, son of Anglican Vicar of Harrow-on-the-Hill. Educated Charterhouse and Oxford. Entered the Church 1893. Ordained ten years later. Professor of Theology at Heythrop. To the Stonyhurst Series, contributed *Natural Theology* and *Principles of Logic*. His *Christian Marriage* is the first book of the Heythrop Theological Series.

KELLY, BLANCHE MARY. Born 1881 in Troy, N. Y. Educated Sacred Heart, Kenwood. Head of Editorial Staff of Catholic Encyclopedia. Has been Professor of English at Mount St. Vincent's College since 1922. Co-editor of Catholic Dictionary. Books published: *Mary the Mother* (1918), *The Valley of Vision* (poem), *Well of English, The Sudden Rose*.

KNOX, MSGR. RONALD. Born 1888, son of the Anglican Bishop of Manchester. Had a brilliant career at Eton and Oxford. Joined the Church in 1917. A Spiritual Aeneid is the story of his conversion. Among his best-known books are *Essays in Satire, Caliban in Grub Street, Broadcast Minds, Memories of the Future, Sanctions, Barchester Pilgrimage* and *Let Dons Delight*. All these are concerned, more or less polemically, with present-day attitudes to religion. *The Mystery of the Kingdom* and *The Rich Young Man* are straightforward spiritual works. Of several detective stories, *The Viaduct Murder* is best known.

LEEN, EDWARD. See page 78.

LE FORT, GERTRUDE VON. See page 116.

LUNN, ARNOLD. Born in Madras, 1888. Educated Harrow and Oxford. In 1921, wrote *Roman Converts*, strongly anti-Catholic in tone. A biography of John Wesley (1928) was followed by *The Flight from Reason*, in which the anti-Catholic tone of *Roman Converts* is considerably modified. Then came two controversies in book form, one with Fr. Ronald Knox, the other with the agnostic C. E. M. Joad. In 1933 he joined the Church. *Now I See* set down some of the reasons.

Since then he has written *Within that City* and *A Saint in the Slave Trade; Science and the Supernatural* (a controversy with J. S. B. Haldane), *Spanish Rehearsal* and *Whither Europe.*

MARITAIN, JACQUES. Born 1885 of Protestant family, grandson of Jules Favre. Studied Philosophy at the Sorbonne. Follower of Bergson. Married a Russian Jewess who shared his philosophic sympathies. In 1905 he and his wife were converted to Catholicism under influence of Léon Bloy. Plunged deep in the study of St. Thomas. Now Professor of Philosophy at the Institut Catholique, Paris. In 1933 lectured at the Universities of Toronto and Chicago. The following works, translated into English are fairly representative: *Three Reformers, An Introduction to Philosophy, Art and Scholasticism, Prayer and Intelligence, The Angelic Doctor, Things that are not Caesar's, Philosophy and Progress, Preface to Metaphysics.*

MARTINDALE, CYRIL CHARLES, S.J. Born 1879. Joined the Church on leaving Harrow, entered S.J. Took the highest classical honors at Oxford. Ordained 1911. Did much work among soldiers during and after the War. Has written almost without ceasing, and has done as much as anyone writing in English to rebuild Catholic apologetic round the doctrines of the Supernatural Life and the Mystical Body. As a selection of his work one might suggest *What are Saints, Does God Matter for Me,* and *Towards Loving the Psalms.*

MAURIAC, FRANÇOIS. See page 32.

McNABB, FR. VINCENT, O.P., S.T.M. Born in 1868. Ordained a priest 1891. Was the Prior of Holy Cross, Leicester, 1910-1914, and Prior of Hawkesyard, Staffs, 1914-1917. S.T.M. in 1917. Chevalier of the Order of the Crown of Belgium 1919: University of London Extension Lecturer. (Westminster Centre), 1929-1934. Author of *Oxford Conferences on Prayer, Oxford Conferences on Faith, Infallibility, The Doctrinal Witness of the Fourth Gospel, The Church and the Land, The Catholic Church and Philosophy, The*

*Craft of Prayer, The Craft of Suffering, Saint John
Fisher, Life of Our Lord.*
NOYES, ALFRED. Born in England, 1880. Educated Exeter
College, Oxford. Made his mark as a poet almost immediately. Gave the Lowell Lectures in America,
1913. Note his epic poem, *The Torchbearers, Tales
of the Mermaid Tavern,* and four volumes of Collected Poems. In prose his outstanding works are *The
Unknown God* (his apologia—he joined the Church
in 1927), *Orchard's Bay* and *Pageant of Letters.*
O'MAHONY, FR. JAMES, O.M.Cap. Born Mitchelstown,
Cork, 1897. Joined Capuchins 1913. Graduated Uni-
versity College, Cork, in 1918. Ordained at Rome
1924. Ph.D. Louvain "avec la plus grande distinction,"
1926. Agrégation 1928, his thesis being *The Desire of
God in the Philosophy of St. Thomas.* 1932-1933,
Deputy Professor of Philosophy, University College,
Cork. Among his books are *Where is Thy God?, The
Franciscans, The Romanticism of Holiness.* He trans-
lated Père Rousselot's *Intellectualisme de St. Thomas.*
PFLEGER, KARL. German Alsatian, born Dachstein 1883.
Educated Hagenau Gymnasium and Strasbourg University, where he made his theological studies at the
Catholic Seminary. After ordination served as curate
in Strasbourg for ten years. 1916 appointed to the
parish of Bilwisheim (now in Bas-Rhin, France).
ROUSSELOT, PIERRE. Born Nantes, 1878. Brilliant
career at Sorbonne, 1894-1895. Jesuit Novice at Canterbury (England). Military service at Nantes, 1899.
Ordained 1908. Same year published *L'Intellectualisme de St. Thomas* (which has been translated
into English) described by Père de Grandmaison, as
perhaps the most penetrating introduction to the
study of Scholastic Philosophy. 1909, Professor of
Theology at Institut Catholique, Paris. 1912, collab-
orated with Fr. Huby, S.J. and others in *Christus,* a
survey of the History of Religions. (His section appears in English as *The Life of the Church*). Served
as sergeant in the War. Killed April 1915. The war

dealt no heavier blow to Catholic theology and philosophy.

SARGENT, DANIEL. A Bostonian. Educated Groton and Harvard. Continued studies in France, where he joined the Church. A close friend of Jacques Maritain. A member of the English faculty of the University of Hard. Has written *Thomas More, Four Independents, Our Land and Our Lady,* and in verse, *The Song of the Three Children.*

SHEEN, MONSIGNOR FULTON J. Born Illinois, May 8th, 1895. Monsignor Sheen graduated from St. Viator College, and was ordained in 1919. After six years of graduate studies in the Universities of Washington, Paris, Louvain and Rome, he received from the two latter universities, respectively, his Ph.D. and D.D. degrees. In 1925 taught Dogmatic Theology in St. Edmund's College, Ware, England, and the following year was aggregated to the faculty of the University of Louvain. In 1926, the University of Louvain awarded him the Cardinal Mercier prize for Philosophy. Holds the chair of Philosophy of Religion at the Catholic University of America, Washington, D. C. Author of *God and Intelligence, The Life of All Living, The Mystical Body of Christ, Whence Come Wars* and many other works.

SUTHERLAND, HALLIDAY GIBSON, M.D. Born Glasgow, 1882. Educated Merchiston Castle School, Glasgow High School and (medically) Universities of Edinburgh, Aberdeen and Dublin; discovered the aetiology of cerebro-spinal fever 1915; had been President of the Tuberculosis Society. Hon. Examining Physician to the Queen Alexandria Sanatorium Fund; Deputy Commns. of Medical Services (Tuberculosis) for South-West England and Wales 1920-1925, Assistant Medical Officer for England County Council 1926. Entered the Church 1919. Has written *The Arches of the Years, A Time to Keep, Laws of Life.*

WALL, BERNARD. Born 1906. Educated Stonyhurst College, Oxford and Fribourg. Founder and editor of *Colosseum* (quarterly) co-editor (with Christopher

Dawson) of *Essays in Order*. Married Barbara Lucas, grand-daughter of Alice Maynell. Has written *Spain of the Spaniards* and *European Notebook*.

WALSH, WILLIAM THOMAS. Made his name with his first book, *Isabella of Spain*. Graduate of Yale, now in his early forties. Professor at Manhattanville, Litt.D. of Fordham. Probably no Catholic American author has ever had so instantaneous a success with the non-Catholic English public. Has since published *Philip II*.

WARD, MAISIE (MARY JOSEPHINE). Daughter of the late Wilfrid Ward, Newman's biographer. Wife of F. J. Sheed. Is the author of *The Wilfrid Wards and the Transition, Saint Bernardino, Father Maturin, a Memoir,* and is the editor of *The Catholic Evidence Training Outlines* and *The English Way*. Is now writing the life of G. K. Chesterton.

WATKIN, EDWARD INGRAM. Born 1888. Educated at St. Paul's School, London, and at Oxford. Joined the Church in 1912. His most notable books are *The Philosophy of Mysticism, The Bow in the Clouds, A Philosophy of Form, Men and Tendencies, The Catholic Centre*.

WAUGH, EVELYN. Educated at Lancing and Hertford College, Oxford. Had instantaneous success as writer of novels. *Decline and Fall* and *Vile Bodies* made him leader of younger English novelists. Joined the Church in 1932. Was war-correspondent in Ethiopian Campaign. Now in the British Army. Has published since his conversion *Black Mischief* and *A Handful of Dust* (novels), *Edmund Campion, Waugh in Abyssinia*.

YEO, MRS. MARGARET. Educated Barton Segrave Rectory, Northants and Lausanne. Received into the Church 1916. Oblate of Prinknash Priory. Has written many novels and articles on the English Martyrs and Confessors under Tudors and Stuarts. Her main books are *Don John of Austria,* and *The Greatest of the Borgias*.

INDEX

Where a page is shown in lighter type, it means that the author or book is merely referred to on that page.